Uninvited

STUDY GUIDE + STREAMING VIDEO

Sarah Bonee

Also by Lysa TerKeurst

The Best Yes

The Best Yes DVD and Study Guide

Unglued

Unglued Devotional

Unglued DVD and Participant's Guide

Becoming More Than a Good Bible Study Girl

Becoming More Than a Good Bible Study Girl DVD and Participant's Guide

Capture Her Heart

Capture His Heart

Made to Crave

Made to Crave Devotional

Made to Crave DVD and Participant's Guide

What Happens When Women Say Yes to God

What Happens When Women Walk in Faith

Who Holds the Key to Your Heart?

Children's

It Will Be Okay

Win or Lose, I Love You

Uninvited

Living Loved When You Feel Less Than,
Left Out, and Lonely

STUDY GUIDE + STREAMING VIDEO

Lysa TerKeurst

New York Times Bestselling Author of *The Best Yes*
with Karen Lee-Thorp

HarperChristian
Resources

Contents

How to Use This Guide

GROUP SIZE

The *Uninvited* video study is designed to be experienced in a group setting such as a Bible study, Sunday school class, or any small group gathering. To ensure everyone has enough time to participate in discussions, it is recommended that large groups break up into smaller groups of four to six people each.

MATERIALS NEEDED

Each participant should have her own *Univited* book and study guide, which includes notes for video segments, directions for activities and discussion questions, as well as personal studies to deepen learning between sessions.

TIMING

The time notations—for example (20 minutes)—indicate the *actual* time of video segments and the *suggested* times for each activity or discussion. For example:

Individual Activity: What I Want to Remember (2 minutes)

Adhering to the suggested times will enable you to complete each session in 90 minutes. If you have only one hour for your meeting, you will need to use fewer questions for discussion.

You may also opt to devote two meetings rather than one to each session. In addition to allowing discussions to be more spacious, this has the added advantage of allowing group members to read related chapters in the *Uninvited* book and to complete the personal study between meetings. In the second meeting, devote the time allotted for watching the video to discussing group members' insights and questions from their reading and personal study.

FACILITATION

Each group should appoint a facilitator who is responsible for starting the video and for keeping track of time during discussions and activities. Facilitators may also read questions aloud and monitor discussions, prompting participants to respond and assuring that everyone has the opportunity to participate.

PERSONAL STUDIES

Maximize the impact of the curriculum with additional study between group sessions. There are six personal studies for each session of *Uninvited*. Except for Session 6, these alternate between days when the emphasis is looking at your life and the Scriptures and days when the emphasis is the book chapters.

Living Loved

Live from a deep assurance that you are fully loved, and you won't find yourself begging others for scraps of love. Live loved.

Recommended reading prior to the meeting:
Uninvited book, chapters 1–3

WELCOME!

Welcome to Session 1 of *Uninvited*. If this is your first time together as a group, take a moment to introduce yourselves to one another before watching the video. Then let's get started!

OPTIONAL DISCUSSION:

Basic Definitions (10 minutes)
Use this discussion if time permits or if your group meets for two hours.
Choose one of the following questions to answer:
If you were to write the definition of *love*, what would it be?
If you were to write the definition of *rejection*, what would it be?

VIDEO:

Living Loved (25 minutes)
Play the video segment for Session 1. As you watch, use the outline below to follow along or take additional notes on anything that stands out to you.

Notes

Jesus' words on the Mount of Beatitudes were a proclamation that He had come and prophecy was being fulfilled.

In the Sermon on the Mount, Jesus announced good news for the poor, the mourning, the rejected. The Messiah has come, and if we remain in Him, we can live loved.

This week's statement to hold on to: Live from a deep assurance that you are fully loved, and you won't find yourself begging others for scraps of love. Live loved.

Rejection never has the final say. With Jesus you are forever safe, accepted, held, loved, invited.

God is in our midst and will quiet us with His love.

The "live loved" quest: To get to a place of stable emotions, stable love instead of a downward spiral in response to circumstances.

When giving is from a heart whose real motivation is what we're hoping to get in return, it's not really love at all.

Living loved is sourced in the quiet daily surrender to the One who loves us.

The ballerina longs most for her instructor's approval. Her daily return to her instructor is the key to her seemingly effortless soaring. Likewise, we need to return often to our Instructor, our Creator. His hand is daily poised to continue making us and to complete the good work He began in us. We need to spend time getting refilled by God in His abundant love.

God waits every day with every answer we need, every comfort we crave, while we're out looking for love everywhere else. God wants us to slow down enough to receive from Him.

"Jesus went up on a mountainside and called to him those he wanted, and they came to him. He appointed twelve that they might *be with him* and that he might send them out to preach and to have authority to drive out demons." (Mark 3:13–15 NIV, emphasis added)

We don't need to manipulate our hearts to feel loved. Instead, we settle in our souls that God created us because He so very much loved the thought of us.

GROUP DISCUSSION:

Video Debrief (5 minutes)

1. What part of the teaching had the most impact on you?

love is placed on you.

Blessedness: What Does the Bible Say? (10 minutes)

If your group meets for two hours, allow 20 minutes for this discussion.

Remember, Jesus giving the Sermon on the Mount is a fulfillment of prophecy, because Isaiah 61:1 says, *"The LORD has anointed me to proclaim good news to the poor"* (NIV). The use of the word "poor" here really means the poor in spirit, or those who are afflicted, humble, meek. Jesus came to tell us that He had good news in the midst of hard realities. Read Matthew 5:1–16 aloud, changing readers every few verses, and listen for the way He speaks to our hearts that are so desperate for acceptance.

¹ Now when Jesus saw the crowds, he went up on a mountainside and sat down. His disciples came to him, ² and he began to teach them.

He said:

³ "Blessed are the poor in spirit,
for theirs is the kingdom of heaven.
⁴ Blessed are those who mourn,
for they will be comforted.
⁵ Blessed are the meek,
for they will inherit the earth.
⁶ Blessed are those who hunger and thirst for righteousness,
for they will be filled.
⁷ Blessed are the merciful,
for they will be shown mercy.
⁸ Blessed are the pure in heart,
for they will see God.
⁹ Blessed are the peacemakers,
for they will be called children of God.
¹⁰ Blessed are those who are persecuted because of righteousness,
for theirs is the kingdom of heaven.

[11] "Blessed are you when people insult you, persecute you and falsely say all kinds of evil against you because of me. [12] Rejoice and be glad, because great is your reward in heaven, for in the same way they persecuted the prophets who were before you.

[13] "You are the salt of the earth. But if the salt loses its saltiness, how can it be made salty again? It is no longer good for anything, except to be thrown out and trampled underfoot.

[14] "You are the light of the world. A town built on a hill cannot be hidden. [15] Neither do people light a lamp and put it under a bowl. Instead they put it on its stand, and it gives light to everyone in the house. [16] In the same way, let your light shine before others, that they may see your good deeds and glorify your Father in heaven. (Matthew 5:1–16 NIV)

2. Who does Jesus say are the blessed? What surprises you about this list?

• Why might we call these people blessed, even though their circumstances might not be producing happy feelings?

"Blessed" translates the Greek word *makarios*. It could be rendered as "happy" or "fortunate" if those words aren't taken in a shallow, emotional way. "*Makarios* is a state of existence in relationship to God in which a person is 'blessed' from God's perspective even when he or she doesn't feel happy or isn't presently experiencing good fortune." Jesus isn't exhorting His hearers to live a life worthy of blessing. He is saying that the people He speaks of are already blessed. "Negative feelings, absence of feelings, or adverse conditions cannot take away the blessedness of those who exist in relationship with God."[1] Jesus is telling His hearers that they can be blessed even when they don't feel good. They can live as loved, blessed people regardless of their circumstances.

---

[1] Michael J. Wilkins, *The NIV Application Commentary: Matthew* (Grand Rapids: Zondervan, 2004), 204.

• In what sense are you blessed right now?

• How would your daily life be different if you lived convinced, deep down, that you are blessed, that the kingdom of heaven belongs to you, that your hunger will be satisfied, that you are loved by the Maker of the universe?

3. Read Matthew 5:11–12.

   [11] "Blessed are you when people insult you, persecute you and falsely say all kinds of evil against you because of me. [12] Rejoice and be glad, because great is your reward in heaven, for in the same way they persecuted the prophets who were before you." (Matthew 5:11–12 NIV)

   • What does God's Word say about times when we feel left out, lonely, or less-than?

4. Read Matthew 5:14–16.

   [14] "You are the light of the world. A town built on a hill cannot be hidden. [15] Neither do people light a lamp and put it under a bowl. Instead they put it on its stand, and it gives light to everyone in the house. [16] In the same way, let your light shine before others, that they may see your good deeds and glorify your Father in heaven." (Matthew 5:14–16 NIV)

   • Do you see yourself as the light of the world? Why or why not? How does your perception of yourself affect how you treat others?

5. On the video, Lysa said that the Creator may have planned the migration of birds for the very moment when He was going to point to the birds to illustrate His message. That's how important His hearers were to Him. Do you believe that God loves you so much that He would do the same for you?

[26] "Look at the birds of the air; they do not sow or reap or store away in barns, and yet your heavenly Father feeds them. Are you not much more valuable than they? [27] Can any one of you by worrying add a single hour to your life?" (Matthew 6:26–27 NIV)

- Write down what this passage says about God's deep love for you.

6. Read Matthew 7:9–12.

[9] "Which of you, if your son asks for bread, will give him a stone? [10] Or if he asks for a fish, will give him a snake? [11] If you, then, though you are evil, know how to give good gifts to your children, how much more will your Father in heaven give good gifts to those who ask him! [12] So in everything, do to others what you would have them do to you, for this sums up the Law and the Prophets." (Matthew 7:9–12 NIV)

What do these verses say about God's love for you?

Living Loved in a Sea of Feelings (10 minutes)

If your group meets for two hours, allow 20 minutes for this discussion.

7. Let's take a small assessment and then look at Zephaniah 3 together. Which of the following experiences, if any, do you have on a regular basis?

   ☑ I am often a slave to my runaway emotions and assumptions.

   ☑ I don't think rejection is currently affecting me, but I have had deep hurts in my past.

   ☑ The moods of other people greatly affect my mood.

   ☑ I easily feel rejected.

   ☑ I'm afraid of telling other people "no" for fear that they may be disappointed in me and eventually reject me.

   ☐ I find myself assuming people are thinking the worst of me.

☑ I have a nagging feeling of disappointment in my soul that I'm aware of when I slow down.

☐ I keep moving fast, and that distracts me, so I honestly don't know what I might be feeling if I got still and quiet.

Too often we allow our rejections to scream louder than the truth of God's Word. Read Zephaniah 3:17 as a group: "The LORD your God is in your midst, a mighty one who will save; he will rejoice over you with gladness; he will quiet you by his love; he will exult over you with loud singing" (ESV).

• What do you think it means to be quieted by God's love?

There are two groups of people this verse can give deep assurance to:

1) Those whose past or present rejections scream so loudly that it's impossible to live loved when they are constantly feeling the sting of others' hurtful words.

2) Those who aren't currently feeling rejected but whose past hurts and rejections are affecting them more than they realize. Or those who are typically confident yet can't understand why they shy away from certain groups of people and situations that give them some sense of not being fully welcomed in as they are.

Either way, here's the assurance: Whether the scripts of rejection are screaming or whispering in your mind, all can be quieted by His love. And not just gentle whispers of love but "loud singing" where God Himself exults over you. He wants His voice of love to be the loudest reality in your life.

This reality doesn't rise and fall on your ability to feel loved. It rises and falls on your belief that He is more powerful than the rejection you've faced. There are things in you that need to be quieted. It's His promises, not your performance, that quiets them.

8. Have you rehashed your hurts more than you've rejoiced in God's love? How can Zephaniah 3:17 help you change that pattern?

• What is a daily way you can dwell in the deep assurance of His love so His voice is the loudest in your life?

Say this out loud together:

"Yes, we're going to **deal** with our rejections, but we're not going to **dwell** on them. We will dwell on the loving declarations of God's love. Therefore, we can live loved."

It's easy to live loved when I feel loved.

But some days I'm just not feeling it.

When life karate chops my feelings into words like *hurt, brushed aside,* and *left out* on Monday and then on Tuesday morning the lady at the gym smirks at me, how in heavens am I supposed to be jolly and not assume the worst? For real, it does not come naturally to me to think in those moments, *Girl, I am not picking up that negative vibe you just laid down, because I* live loved.

No way, no how.

I'm going to get in a funk, because that's what I do. I will feel put off, and then I will put on that ratty robe of rejection and wear it all day long.

But I don't want to keep being a slave to my runaway emotions and assumptions. I don't want my days to be dictated by the moods of other people. And I really don't want the rejections of my past feeding my propensity to feel rejected today.

I want the kind of emotional stability I read about in the Bible: "The LORD your God is in your midst, a mighty one who will save; he will rejoice over you with gladness; he will quiet you by his love; he will exult over you with loud singing" (Zephaniah 3:17 ESV).

I love the thought that God is in our midst and that He will quiet me by His love.

Yes, please. I'll take an extra-large order of that every morning.

I want to believe it's possible for me not just in the middle of Bible study but in the middle of life.

So I decided to go on a "live loved" quest. I determined to be a one-woman experiment in whether or not it is actually possible to live from a place of being loved. I wanted to get to a place where my immediate reaction to off-kilter interactions with others wasn't a downward spiral of wonky feelings, but stable love instead.

Uninvited, pages 32–33

This week's statement to hold on to: Live from a deep assurance that you are fully loved, and you won't find yourself begging others for scraps of love. Live loved.

9. Think about the past twenty-four hours. What got in the way of your living loved? Did anything help you live loved? If so, what?

10. What mental picture represents living loved to you?

11. On the video, Lysa said we can be like the ballerina who moves with such grace that she seems to fly because she returns every day to her instructor, who in love tweaks and trains her in the quiet studio. Jesus promises to be our Instructor. He promises to continue His good work in us until it is completed (Philippians 1:6). How is His love training you? What part do we play in the training process? Consider the passages in the quotation box below.

I needed to reconnect with the One who knows how to breathe life and love back into depleted and dead places. Jesus doesn't participate in the rat race. He's into the slower rhythms of life like abiding, delighting, and dwelling—all words used to describe us being with Him.

> "If you abide in Me, and My words abide in you, ask whatever you wish, and it will be done for you" (John 15:7 NASB).

> "Delight yourself in the LORD, and he will give you the desires of your heart" (Psalm 37:4 ESV).

> "He who dwells in the secret place of the Most High shall remain stable *and* fixed under the shadow of the Almighty [Whose power no foe can withstand]" (Psalm 91:1 AMP).

Did you catch the beautiful filling promised in each of those verses? When we abide, delight, and dwell in Him, He then places within us desires that line up with His best desire for us. Therefore, He can give us whatever we ask, because we will only want what's consistent with His best. He can fully satisfy our hearts, because they are consistent with His heart. He can promise us stability, because we're tapped into His consistent power.

Uninvited, pages 37–38

12. Lysa says, "Living loved is sourced in the quiet daily surrender to the One who loves us." Write down some ways that you might go about that quiet daily surrender. What actions are involved? What attitudes are displayed?

How dangerous it is when our soul is gasping for God but we're too distracted flirting with the world to notice. Flirting will give you brief surges of fun feelings but will never really pull you in and hold you close. Indeed, the world entices our flesh but never embraces our soul. All the while, the only love caring enough to embrace us and complete enough to fill us, waits. . . .

We just have to turn to Him. And sit with Him. No matter what. Even if our toes bloody from the constant wear and tear from desperately running to Him. Get to Him daily.

How it must break His heart when we walk around so desperate for a love He waits to give us each and every day.

Uninvited, pages 35–36

OPTIONAL INDIVIDUAL ACTIVITY AND DISCUSSION:

Flirting with the World (20 minutes)

If your group meets for two hours, include this activity as part of your meeting. Allow 20 minutes total—5 minutes for the individual activity and 15 minutes for the group discussion.

Individual Activity (5 minutes)

Complete this activity on your own.

1. Read the excerpt from the *Uninvited* book above. Review the past forty-eight hours of your life and make some notes about times when you flirted with the world. For example, consider times when you:

   ☐ Gave the first moments of your day to things other than checking in with what God might say to you in His Word

   ☐ Checked your social media to see how many likes you had received on your posts

   ☐ Watched television programs or advertisements that stimulated unreasonable desires in you for possessions, romance, or achievement

☐ Worried about problems, talked to people about them, and tried to solve them yourself, instead of praying about them

☐ Bought products you didn't really need

☐ Interacted with another person with a goal of getting his or her approval

These notes are just for you; you won't have to share them with the group unless you choose to do so.

2. What do you typically do or turn to when you don't feel loved?

Group Discussion (15 minutes)

1. How do you tend to feel after you've been flirting with the world?

2. What do we do if flirting with the world feels good but spending time with the Lord feels dry?

The irony is that flirting with the world ultimately leaves us empty, even though it can feel good at the time. The only thing that truly nourishes our souls is the love of God. If you've been flirting with the world, take heart. As we go further in the study, you'll find yourself developing the habit of living loved, and the world won't seem so compelling.

3. How can you live loved this week? What is one step you can take toward that goal?

Becoming a Group that Lives Loved (8 minutes)

If your group meets for two hours, allow 18 minutes for this discussion.

13. The five remaining sessions in *Uninvited* will take you further on the path toward living loved instead of stumbling down the road of rejection. In addition to learning together as a group, it's important to be aware of how God is at work among you in the time you spend together—especially in how you relate to one another and share your lives throughout the study. As you discuss the teaching in each session, there will be many opportunities to speak life-giving—and life-challenging—words, and to listen to one another deeply.

Take a few moments to consider the kinds of things that are important to you in this setting. What do you need or want from the other members of the group? Use one or more of the sentence starters below, or your own statement, to help the group understand the best way to be good companions to you throughout this *Uninvited* study. As each person responds, use the chart on pages 22–23 to briefly note what is important to that person and how you can support and encourage her.

It really helps me when . . .

I tend to withdraw or feel anxious when . . .

I'd like you to challenge me about . . .

I'll know this group is a safe place if you . . .

In our discussions, the best thing you could do for me is . . .

NAME	THE BEST WAY I CAN ENCOURAGE AND HELP THIS PERSON IS . . .

NAME	THE BEST WAY I CAN ENCOURAGE AND HELP THIS PERSON IS . . .

INDIVIDUAL ACTIVITY:

What I Want to Remember (2 minutes)

Complete this activity on your own.

1. Briefly review the outline and any notes you took.
2. In the space below, write down the most significant thing you gained in this session—from the teaching, activities, or discussions.

   What I want to remember from this session . . .

(If you want to share what you're learning and see what others are saying about *Uninvited* on social media, use the hashtag #Uninvitedbook!)

CLOSING PRAYER

Close your time together with prayer. Share your prayer requests with one another. Ask God to help you hear His good news for the poor in spirit, to help you know in your heart of hearts that you are blessed right now, no matter what other people say or do. Ask Him to help you lived loved as you go through your day.

BETWEEN-SESSIONS PERSONAL STUDIES

Every session in *Uninvited* includes six days of personal study to help you make meaningful connections between your life and what you're learning each week. In this first week, you'll start observing times when you feel rejection so that you can eventually notice patterns in your experience and responses. You'll also have a chance to read the chapters of the *Uninvited* book that relate to this week's teachings. You'll alternate between days when the emphasis is looking at your life and the Scriptures and days when the emphasis is the book chapters.

Personal Study

DAY 1: STUDY AND REFLECT

1. Feelings of rejection come from disappointment. We want to receive one message, but we get another. We want people to tell us they love us and want what we have to offer, but they send (or seem to send) the opposite message.

   To stay centered in God's love even when we're rejected, it's helpful to start by paying conscious attention to the messages of rejection we have received. We need to know the kinds of situations that have led us to feel rejected, and we need to know the messages we have heard from those situations.

   In the chart that follows, record your major experiences of rejection, whether as a child, a teen, or an adult. (You will have opportunity to add new notes to this chart as the week progresses.)

WHO SENT THE REJECTING MESSAGE?	WHAT WAS THE MESSAGE YOU RECEIVED?	ON A SCALE OF 1 TO 5 (5 BEING THE WORST), HOW PAINFUL WAS THE MESSAGE?
Examples:		
My mother	She was preoccupied with caring for my sick brother and so didn't make time to be with me or listen to me. I got the message, "Your brother is important, but you're not."	5
My boss	He praised a colleague's work but overlooked my contribution. I got the message, "You don't count. You're invisible. Your contribution isn't valued."	3

WHO SENT THE REJECTING MESSAGE?	WHAT WAS THE MESSAGE YOU RECEIVED?	ON A SCALE OF 1 TO 5 (5 BEING THE WORST), HOW PAINFUL WAS THE MESSAGE?

2. How would you summarize the overall message you have received from your experiences of rejection?

Negative self-talk was a rejection from my past that I had allowed to settle into the core of who I am. I talked about myself in ways I would never let another person. Hints of self-rejection laced my thoughts and poisoned my words more than I cared to admit.

Self-rejection paves the landing strip for the rejection of others to arrive and pull on up to the gates of our hearts. Think about why it hurts so much when other people say or do things that make you feel rejected. Isn't it in part due to the fact they just voiced some vulnerability you've already berated yourself for?

It hurts exponentially more when you're kicked in an already bruised shin.

Uninvited, page 7

3. When have you gone into an encounter at work or church or somewhere else with the messages of self-rejection already braced to make you feel like an outsider?

4. You're not stuck with those messages of self-rejection forever. To overcome the effects of rejection, you can rehearse the truth of God's Word until it replaces any negative thoughts or feelings. For instance, if you are struggling with the message that you don't matter, then a passage like Ephesians 1:4–5 would be helpful to rehearse:

[4] Even before he made the world, God loved us and chose us in Christ to be holy and without fault in his eyes. [5] God decided in advance to adopt us into his own family by bringing us to himself through Jesus Christ. This is what he wanted to do, and it gave him great pleasure. (NLT)

Copy this passage below, using the word "me" in place of "us" to personalize it for yourself.

Now read the personalized version aloud.

Write the personalized version someplace where you will see it during the day. For example, put it on your phone so that you can glance at it frequently. Ask God to write this verse on your heart so that you will believe it and live by it. If you really want to overcome strong messages of rejection, make a plan to read aloud the personalized passage five times a day for the next seven days. Read it aloud with conviction.

Write out a prayer to God using Ephesians 1:4–5 as a basis. "Loving Father, please help me to know that . . ."

My whole life I've searched for a love to satisfy the deepest longings within me to be known, treasured, and wholly accepted. When You created me, Lord, Your very first thought of me made Your heart explode with a love that set You in pursuit of me. Your love for me was so great that You, the God of the whole universe, went on a personal quest to woo me, adore me, and finally grab hold of me with the whisper, "I will never let you go."

Lord, I release my grip on all the things I was holding on to, preventing me from returning Your passionate embrace. I want nothing to hold me but You.

So, with breathless wonder, I give You all of my faith, all of my hope, and all of my love.

I picture myself carrying the old torn-out boards that inadequately propped me up and place them in a pile. This pile contains other things I can remove from me now that my new intimacy-based identity is established.

I lay down my need to understand why things happen the way they do.

I lay down my fears about others I love walking away.

I lay down my desire to prove my worth.

I lay down my resistance to fully trust Your thoughts, Your ways, and Your plans, Lord.

I lay down my anger, unforgiveness, and stubborn ways that beg me to build walls when I sense hints of rejection.

I lay all these things down with my broken boards and ask that Your holy fire consume them until they become weightless ashes.

And as I walk away, my soul feels safe. Held. And truly free to finally be me.

Uninvited, pages 25–26

DAY 2: READ AND LEARN

If you have an experience of rejection, record it on the chart on pages 25–26. Be sure to write down the message you took away from the experience. Also, read aloud your personalized version of Ephesians 1:4–5 several times during the day.

Review chapters 1–3 of the *Uninvited* book. Use the space below to note any insights or questions you want to bring to the next group session.

DAY 3: STUDY AND REFLECT

Continue to make notes about your experiences of rejection on the chart on pages 25–26. Read aloud your personalized version of Ephesians 1:4–5 a few times during the day.

1. Isaiah 61:1–11 is a powerhouse of promises that Jesus Christ is fulfilling for you. Feast for a moment on this passage:

> [1] The Spirit of the Sovereign LORD is on me,
> because the LORD has anointed me
> to proclaim good news to the poor.
> He has sent me to bind up the brokenhearted,
> to proclaim freedom for the captives
> and release from darkness for the prisoners,
> [2] to proclaim the year of the LORD's favor
> and the day of vengeance of our God,
> to comfort all who mourn,
> [3] and provide for those who grieve in Zion—
> to bestow on them a crown of beauty
> instead of ashes,
> the oil of joy
> instead of mourning,
> and a garment of praise
> instead of a spirit of despair.

They will be called oaks of righteousness,
    a planting of the LORD
    for the display of his splendor.
[4] They will rebuild the ancient ruins
    and restore the places long devastated;
they will renew the ruined cities
    that have been devastated for generations.
[5] Strangers will shepherd your flocks;
    foreigners will work your fields and vineyards.
[6] And you will be called priests of the LORD,
    you will be named ministers of our God.
You will feed on the wealth of nations,
    and in their riches you will boast.
[7] Instead of your shame
    you will receive a double portion,
and instead of disgrace
    you will rejoice in your inheritance.
And so you will inherit a double portion in your land,
    and everlasting joy will be yours.
[8] "For I, the LORD, love justice;
    I hate robbery and wrongdoing.
In my faithfulness I will reward my people
    and make an everlasting covenant with them.
[9] Their descendants will be known among the nations
    and their offspring among the peoples.
All who see them will acknowledge
    that they are a people the LORD has blessed."
[10] I delight greatly in the LORD;
    my soul rejoices in my God.
For he has clothed me with garments of salvation
    and arrayed me in a robe of his righteousness,
as a bridegroom adorns his head like a priest,
    and as a bride adorns herself with her jewels.
[11] For as the soil makes the sprout come up
    and a garden causes seeds to grow,
so the Sovereign LORD will make righteousness
    and praise spring up before all nations. (NIV)

- Review verses 1–7 and circle the phrase "instead of" every time it appears.

- Use those same promises to fill in the blanks here so you can be reminded of what Jesus will fulfill in you:

Crown of_____ instead of _____

Oil of_____ instead of _____

Garment of_____ instead of _____

Instead of your _____ you will receive a _____

Instead of _____ you will rejoice in _____

- Review Isaiah 61:10 and write it out below as a declaration of truth in your life.

- Go back through Isaiah 61:2b–9 and write below additional promises that you long to see fulfilled in your life. (Example from verse 4: He will rebuild and restore my devastated places.)

- How can truly believing that Jesus came to fulfill Isaiah 61 help you to live loved all day, every day?

2. What makes Isaiah 61 possible is the reality of Isaiah 53. We'll make notes about this later this week, but for now, read Isaiah 53 with a heart of thanksgiving.

DAY 4: READ AND LEARN

Continue to make notes about any experiences of rejection on the chart on pages 25–26. Read aloud your personalized version of Ephesians 1:4–5 a few times during the day.

Read chapter 4 of the *Uninvited* book, "Alone in a Crowded Room." Use the space below to note any insights or questions you want to bring to the next group session.

DAY 5: STUDY AND REFLECT

Continue to make notes about any experiences of rejection on the chart on pages 25–26. Read aloud your personalized version of Ephesians 1:4–5 a few times during the day.

Jesus knows what it's like to be rejected. He came into the world to save His people, but they rejected and ultimately crucified Him. Here is Isaiah's prophecy concerning Him:

> ³He was despised and rejected by mankind,
>   a man of suffering, and familiar with pain.
> Like one from whom people hide their faces
>   he was despised, and we held him in low esteem.
> ⁴Surely he took up our pain
>   and bore our suffering,
> yet we considered him punished by God,
>   stricken by him, and afflicted.
> ⁵But he was pierced for our transgressions,
>   he was crushed for our iniquities;
> the punishment that brought us peace was on him,
>   and by his wounds we are healed. (Isaiah 53:3–5 NIV)

1. How did Jesus experience rejection during His earthly life? See, for example, Mark 2:23–3:6 and 3:20–22.

2. Go through the Isaiah 53 passage and circle words or phrases that indicate His suffering. List those below.

3. Who did Jesus suffer for and what did that punishment bring to us? Fill in the blanks below.

   He took up _____ pain (v. 4) and bore _____ suffering (v. 4)
   He was pierced for _____ transgressions (v. 5)
   He was crushed for _____ iniquities (v. 5)

Something to note:

Our pain and suffering are often brought on by things done *to* us.

But transgressions (meaning willful disobedience) and iniquities (meaning continued disobedience without repentance) are things done *by* us.

   Jesus covered it all—all that has been done *to* us and *by* us.

   His punishment brought us _____ (v. 5)
   His wounds brought us _____ (v. 5)

4. Jesus knows our heart, our feelings, our past, our emotions. But sometimes it's helpful to just acknowledge those thoughts and feelings. Take a few minutes to tell Jesus about your experiences of rejection. Tell Him the messages you have received and how they make you feel.

   After you've been thoroughly honest with Him, thank Him for His willingness to become human and suffer rejection on your behalf. Thank Him for forgiving the times you have rejected Him. Allow Him to minister to your soul in the place of your pain, and allow yourself to experience His forgiveness. You can write your prayer here.

DAY 6:   READ AND LEARN

Continue to make notes about your experiences of rejection on the chart on pages 25–26. Read aloud your personalized version of Ephesians 1:4–5 at least three times during the day.

Read chapter 5 of the *Uninvited* book, "Hello, My Name Is Trust Issues." Use the space below to note any insights or questions you want to bring to the next group session.

Empty or Full?

I can choose to bring my emptiness or
God's fullness into any situation I face.

GROUP DISCUSSION:

Checking In (5 minutes)

If your group meets for two hours, allow 15 minutes for this discussion.

Welcome to Session 2 of *Uninvited*. A key part of getting to know God better is sharing your journey with others. Before watching the video, briefly check in with one another about your experience since the last session. For example:

- What insights did you discover in the personal study or in chapters 1–5 of the *Uninvited* book?

- How did the last session affect your daily life or your relationship with God?

VIDEO:

Empty or Full? (15 minutes)

Play the video segment for Session 2. As you watch, use the outline provided to follow along or to take additional notes on anything that stands out to you.

Notes

This week's statement to hold on to: I can choose to bring my emptiness or God's fullness into any situation I face.

I don't want life's unpredictable circumstances to make my mindset full of unnecessary rejection.

Peter cut off the ear of one of the high priest's servants. Jesus healed the man (Luke 22:49–51). In the middle of His most desperate rejection, Jesus had compassion on one of His persecutors.

Peter denied Jesus three times (Luke 22:54–62). What might have happened if Peter hadn't been afraid of being rejected by the servant girl? What if Peter had determined to bring the fullness of God into the situation? Instead he brought his emptiness.

Jesus asked Peter, "Do you love me more than these?" (John 21:15 NIV). We all have our things we choose over Jesus.

Jesus told Peter: "Feed my lambs," "Take care of my sheep," and "Feed my sheep" (John 21:15–17 NIV). This is the pattern of the Bedouin shepherd. Jesus was trying to turn Peter from a fisherman into a shepherd. In this next season of his life, Peter would have to be slower and gentler in caring for people like a shepherd.

Do you walk into situations like a shepherd, eager to love Jesus more than these, free to look for ways to bless others? Or do you walk in looking for ways for others to bless you? Bring an inviting spirit to fill the room with the loving presence of God. Feed the lambs. It's our choice. We can bring the fullness or the emptiness. Each day is a new day, deciding not to live uninvited but to live in God's fullness.

GROUP DISCUSSION:

Video Debrief (5 minutes)

1. What part of the teaching had the most impact on you?

Feed My Sheep (10 minutes)

If your group meets for two hours, allow 20 minutes for this discussion.

2. Read Luke 22:47–53.

   47 While he was still speaking a crowd came up, and the man who was called Judas, one of the Twelve, was leading them. He approached Jesus to kiss him, 48 but Jesus asked him, "Judas, are you betraying the Son of Man with a kiss?"
   49 When Jesus' followers saw what was going to happen, they said, "Lord, should we strike with our swords?" 50 And one of them struck the servant of the high priest, cutting off his right ear.
   51 But Jesus answered, "No more of this!" And he touched the man's ear and healed him.
   52 Then Jesus said to the chief priests, the officers of the temple guard, and the elders, who had come for him, "Am I leading a rebellion, that you have come with swords and clubs? 53 Every day I was with you in the temple courts, and you did not lay a hand on me. But this is your hour—when darkness reigns." (Luke 22:47–53 NIV)

- How was it possible for Jesus to pay attention to the needs of one of His enemies and heal the man's ear in the midst of such a terrible betrayal?

3. Read Luke 22:54–62.

⁵⁴ Then seizing him, they led him away and took him into the house of the high priest. Peter followed at a distance. ⁵⁵ And when some there had kindled a fire in the middle of the court-yard and had sat down together, Peter sat down with them. ⁵⁶ A servant girl saw him seated there in the firelight. She looked closely at him and said, "This man was with him."

⁵⁷ But he denied it. "Woman, I don't know him," he said.

⁵⁸ A little later someone else saw him and said, "You also are one of them."

"Man, I am not!" Peter replied.

⁵⁹ About an hour later another asserted, "Certainly this fellow was with him, for he is a Galilean."

⁶⁰ Peter replied, "Man, I don't know what you're talking about!" Just as he was speaking, the rooster crowed. ⁶¹ The Lord turned and looked straight at Peter. Then Peter remembered the word the Lord had spoken to him: "Before the rooster crows today, you will disown me three times." ⁶² And he went outside and wept bitterly. (Luke 22:54–62 NIV)

- What might Peter have done differently if he had been living from a place of God's fullness in this scene? What might have been the results?

4. Read John 21:15–17.

¹⁵ When they had finished eating, Jesus said to Simon Peter, "Simon son of John, do you love me more than these?"

"Yes, Lord," he said, "you know that I love you."

Jesus said, "Feed my lambs."

¹⁶ Again Jesus said, "Simon son of John, do you love me?"

He answered, "Yes, Lord, you know that I love you."

Jesus said, "Take care of my sheep."

¹⁷ The third time he said to him, "Simon son of John, do you love me?"

Peter was hurt because Jesus asked him the third time, "Do you love me?" He said, "Lord, you know all things; you know that I love you."

Jesus said, "Feed my sheep." (John 21:15–17 NIV)

• Jesus asked Peter, "Do you love me more than these?" We all have our things that we choose over Jesus. What are "these" in your life?

• Who are the lambs and sheep that Jesus asks you to feed? How can you feed them?

5. Think of a recent situation when you had a choice to walk into it full of Christ, living loved and looking for ways to bless others, or to walk in looking for others to bless you in your emptiness. Which choice did you make? What were the results?

• What would you do differently next time, if anything?

Filled with God's Fullness: What Does the Bible Say? (15 minutes)

If your group meets for two hours, allow 25 minutes for this discussion.

Don't be hard on yourself if you tend to enter situations burdened with your own emptiness. There's hope! You really can change your habit in this area. This week's statement to hold on to is, "I can choose to bring my emptiness or God's fullness into any situation I face." How can you know that God's fullness is really available to you? Because the apostle Paul says so. This is what he prays for his readers:

> [14] For this reason I kneel before the Father, [15] from whom every family in heaven and on earth derives its name. [16] I pray that out of his glorious riches he may strengthen you with power through his Spirit in your inner being, [17] so that Christ may dwell in your hearts through faith. And I pray that you, being rooted and established in love, [18] may have power, together with all the Lord's holy people, to grasp how wide and long and high and deep is the love of Christ, [19] and to know this love that surpasses knowledge—that you may be filled to the measure of all the fullness of God. (Ephesians 3:14–19 NIV)

6. Paul prays that you will be strengthened with power through the Holy Spirit in your inner being (v. 16). What will that accomplish (v. 17a)? Why is this important?

• What do you think are some of the things that are possible for us to do only when we are strengthened with power through the Spirit? What can't we do without that strengthening?

• Paul prays for power again in verse 18. What power does he ask for this time?

• What will that power accomplish (v. 19)?

• Why do you need to grasp the breadth and depth of Christ's love?

• Pause and read Paul's prayer out loud together as a group (page 39).

7. Read the following excerpt from the *Uninvited* book.

I grasp the love of Christ.

I sense when I'm making choices that don't reflect God's love.

I'm disgusted by those choices.

I am willing to tell my flesh no.

I'm just not sure *how* to tell my flesh no. . . .

We have the power through Christ, who is over every power, including the pull of the flesh and the sting of rejection. When we have Christ, we are full—fully loved and accepted and fully empowered to say no.

This is true on the days we feel it and still true when we don't feel Jesus' love at all. If we live rooted and established in His love, we don't just have knowledge of His love in our minds, but it becomes a reality that anchors us. Though winds of hurt and rejection blow, they cannot uproot us and rip us apart. His love holds us. His love grounds us. His love is a glorious weight preventing the harsh words and hurtful situations from being a destructive force. We feel the wind but aren't destroyed by it. This is the "fullness of God" mentioned in the verse from Ephesians 3 that we just read.

There is power in really knowing this. This isn't dependent on what you've accomplished. Or on another person loving you or accepting you. Nor is it because you always feel full. You are full, because Christ brought the fullness to you.

Yes, I am fully loved, fully accepted, and fully empowered to say no to my flesh. Speak that truth in the power He's given you. Believe that truth in the power He's given you. Live that truth in the power He's given you.

Uninvited, pages 48, 49–50

- Why is it important to know that you are filled with the fullness of God even when you don't feel it?

OPTIONAL INDIVIDUAL ACTIVITY AND DISCUSSION:

Chasing Things to Make Us Full (20 minutes)

If your group meets for two hours, include this activity as part of your meeting. Allow 20 minutes total—5 minutes for the individual activity and 15 minutes for the group discussion.

Individual Activity (5 minutes)

Complete this activity on your own.

1. Read the excerpt from the *Uninvited* book on page 43. Take a few minutes to review your life and ask yourself if you have been chasing anything instead of God to make you feel full. Do you look to your work, your family, another relationship, a possession, or something else hoping it will ease your emptiness? Write some notes here.

2. Do you have trouble sitting quietly with God because a sense of emptiness rushes in? What is it like for you to sit quietly? Practice the discipline of Psalm 46:10 ("Be still, and know that I am God") for a couple of minutes and notice what happens inside you. Don't be hard on yourself if stillness doesn't come easily to you. Just gently observe what happens to you, and redirect your attention to the verse, "Be still, and know that I am God."

Group Discussion (15 minutes)

1. What was it like for you to sit quietly? Did you find yourself able to focus, or did your mind buzz with distractions? Is quietness a welcome break or an uncomfortable void?

2. Were you able to identify anything you chase to ease your emptiness? If so, share it if you feel comfortable doing so. What do you want to do about it?

3. Paul says in Philippians 4:12, "I have learned the secret of being content in any and every situation" (NIV). What will help you get to a place where you can say those words with

conviction? What could get in the way? What can you do about those potential obstacles so that you can make progress?

But here's the one thing we must watch out for: If we become enamored with something in this world we think offers better fullness than God, we will make room for it. We leak out His fullness to make room for something else we want to chase.

It will happen if you chase a guy you think will make you more full.

It will happen if you chase an opportunity you think will make you more full.

It will happen if you chase some possession you think will make you more full.

It will happen if you, like me, chase perfect order from an imperfect world thinking it will make you more full.

But at some point every one of those things will reveal its absolute inability to keep us full.

And then, since we denied God's power to lead us, we forget His power to hold us. So in an effort not to freefall, we chase something or someone else we think will ease our emptiness.

David takes a different approach.

He reminds himself at the end of this psalm [23:6 NIV] of trust and fulfillment, "Surely your goodness and love will follow me / all the days of my life, / and I will dwell in the house of the LORD / forever."

There is a certainty in what David is declaring here.

It's not based on a feeling or a good circumstance. It's based on what David knows to be unchanging truth.

Uninvited, pages 63–64

Becoming a Group that Lives Loved (8 minutes)

If your group meets for two hours, allow 18 minutes for this discussion.

8. At the end of the group discussion for Session 1, you had the opportunity to share what you need from other members of the group and to write down the best ways you can be good companions to one another (pages 21–23).

- Briefly restate what you asked for from the group in Session 1. What additions or clarifications would you like to make that would help the group know more about how to be a good companion to you? As each person responds, add any additional information to the chart on pages 22–23. (If you were absent from the last session, share you response to question 13 on page 21. Then use the chart to write down what is important to each member of the group.)

- In what ways, if any, did you find yourself responding differently to other group members in this session based on what they asked for in the previous session? What made that easy or difficult for you to do?

INDIVIDUAL ACTIVITY:

What I Want to Remember (2 minutes)
Complete this activity on your own.

1. Briefly review the outline and any notes you took.

2. In the space below, write down the most significant thing you gained in this session—from the teaching, activities, or discussions.

   What I want to remember from this session . . .

(If you want to share what you're learning and see what others are saying about *Uninvited* on social media, use the hashtag #Uninvitedbook!)

CLOSING PRAYER

Close your time together with prayer. Share your prayer requests with one another. Ask God again to strengthen all of you with power in your inner being and to give you the power to grasp how wide and long and high and deep is the love of Christ, so that you may be filled with the fullness of God.

Personal Study

DAY 1: STUDY AND REFLECT

1. If you have any experiences of rejection this week, write them here.

WHO SENT THE REJECTING MESSAGE?	WHAT WAS THE MESSAGE YOU RECEIVED?	ON A SCALE OF 1 TO 5 (5 BEING THE WORST), HOW PAINFUL WAS THE MESSAGE?

2. Experiences of rejection don't cause the same feelings in everyone. It's helpful to put words to the feelings you have when you experience rejection. Look back at what you wrote in question 1 of Session 1's personal study on pages 25–26, as well as question 1 of today's personal study. Think about these experiences of rejection—both the recent ones and the ones from farther in the past—and in each case name the feeling it evoked in you. You can write the feeling right on the chart or in the margin. Here are some possible feelings related to rejection:

sad	hopeless	defeated
angry	helpless	damaged
lonely	vengeful	inferior
aching	loss	brokenhearted
left out	doubting	overlooked
inadequate (not good enough)		

3. What patterns do you see in your feelings? For example, maybe in the past you felt help-less and in the recent experiences you felt helpless too. Or maybe as a child you tended to feel helpless but today experiences of rejection make you feel angry or vengeful. Or maybe you see a pattern of growth in yourself, where anger was your dominant emotion in the past but now you only feel sadness when rejected.

4. How do you compensate for rejection in healthy and unhealthy ways?

5. Did reflecting on Ephesians 1:4–5 help you think differently about your experiences of rejection? If so, how? If not, did it have any other effects?

6. Offer a prayer to God that reflects your feelings about rejection and also what you know is true about Him. For example:

Lord, thank You that You are eager to strengthen me with power in my inner being, to root and ground me in love, to enable me to grasp the vastness of Your love, to fill me with Your fullness. I have been feeling _____ about my experiences of rejection. But because of You, my feelings are shifting . . .

And I know my feelings aren't the whole story about my experiences, because You . . .

Please strengthen me with power through Your Spirit in my inner being. Please root and ground me in love, so that I can grasp how wide and long and high and deep Your love is, even though it surpasses knowledge, so that I may be filled with your fullness.

DAY 2: READ AND LEARN

Continue to make notes about your experiences of rejection on the chart on page 45.

Read chapter 6 of the *Uninvited* book, "Friendship Breakups." Use the space below to note any insights or questions you want to bring to the next group session.

DAY 3: STUDY AND REFLECT

1. You may continue to have experiences of rejection, but one way to keep them from dominating you is to choose to bring God's fullness into every situation you encounter. So now, for the rest of this week, keep track of opportunities to bring God's fullness into situations. Make note of whether you seized or missed that opportunity and how you felt about the situation afterward.

SITUATION	DID I BRING GOD'S FULLNESS?	WHAT HAPPENED AND HOW I FELT
Examples:		
Gathering after church	Yes	*I saw someone alone whom I didn't know, and I had the courage to go up to that person and introduce myself. She wasn't terribly responsive, but she did say she was new to the church and appreciated being greeted. I felt awkward during the conversation, but afterward I felt proud of myself for taking the initiative. I knew I had done the right thing even though it wasn't easy. I had resisted the temptation to try to get her to fill me. Instead, I had focused on bringing God's fullness to her.*

SITUATION	DID I BRING GOD'S FULLNESS?	WHAT HAPPENED AND HOW I FELT

2. What helps you walk into a situation bringing God's fullness? How do you daily prepare to bring the fullness of God? How can you make those preparations a bigger part of your life?

3. What potentially hinders you from walking into situations with God's fullness? How can you make those things that empty you a smaller part of your life?

If we grasp the full love of Christ, we won't grab at other things to fill us. Or if we do, we'll sense it. We'll feel a prick in our spirit when our flesh makes frenzied swipes at happiness, compromising clutches for attention, paranoid assumptions with no facts, joyless attempts to one-up another, and small-minded statements of pride. We'll sense these things, and we'll be disgusted enough to at least pause.

In this pause lies the greatest daily choice we can make. Am I willing to tell my flesh no, so that I can say yes to the fullness of God in this situation?

Uninvited, page 48

4. Choose one of the following verses for reflection this week. Write it someplace where you will see it multiple times a day. Try to read it aloud several times each day.

What, then, shall we say in response to these things? If God is for us, who can be against us? (Romans 8:31 NIV)

For God has said, "I will never fail you. I will never abandon you." So we can say with confidence, "The LORD is my helper, so I will have no fear. What can mere people do to me?" (Hebrews 13:5b–6 NLT)

The LORD is my light and my salvation / —whom shall I fear? / The LORD is the stronghold of my life / —of whom shall I be afraid? (Psalm 27:1 NIV)

5. Pray for God's fullness.

God, thank You for giving me the choice to walk in my emptiness or in Your vast fullness. The main challenge I have in walking in Your fullness is . . .

Please empower me to overcome that. Please strengthen me with power through Your Spirit in my inner being. Please root and ground me in love, so that I can grasp how wide and long and high and deep Your love is, even though it surpasses knowledge, so that I may be filled with Your fullness.

DAY 4: READ AND LEARN

Continue to make notes about entering situations in God's fullness or your own emptiness on pages 48–49.

Read chapter 7 of the *Uninvited* book, "When Our Normal Gets Snatched." Use the space below to note any insights or questions you want to bring to the next group session.

DAY 5: STUDY AND REFLECT

Continue to make notes about entering situations in God's fullness or your own emptiness on pages 48–49.

1. In Ephesians 3, Paul prays that you will grasp how broad and wide and high and deep is the love of Christ that surpasses knowledge. Grasping that will enable you to be filled with the fullness of God. So it's helpful to reflect on Christ's love and allow the wonder of it to captivate your mind.

   That love was shown most profoundly when He allowed Himself to be crucified on your behalf. So take some time today to reflect on the love of Christ expressed through the crucifixion. Read Matthew 27:32–50. Try to put yourself into the scene. See the sights, hear the sounds, feel the physical pain, smell the smells, and taste the tastes. Wine mixed with gall is bitter but could take the edge off pain. Wine vinegar is tart and acidic. Imagine watching a man you love be nailed to a wooden crossbeam and hoisted into the air. Hear the voices of the other onlookers—what do they say? What do you feel as the scene unfolds?

[32] As they were going out, they met a man from Cyrene, named Simon, and they forced him to carry the cross. [33] They came to a place called Golgotha (which means "the place of the skull"). [34] There they offered Jesus wine to drink, mixed with gall; but after tasting it, he refused to drink it. [35] When they had crucified him, they divided up his clothes by casting lots. [36] And sitting down, they kept watch over him there. [37] Above his head they placed the written charge against him: THIS IS JESUS, THE KING OF THE JEWS.

[38] Two rebels were crucified with him, one on his right and one on his left. [39] Those who passed by hurled insults at him, shaking their heads [40] and saying, "You who are going to destroy the temple and build it in three days, save yourself! Come down from the cross, if you are the Son of God!" [41] In the same way the chief priests, the teachers of the law and the elders mocked him. [42] "He saved others," they said, "but he can't save himself! He's the king of Israel! Let him come down now from the cross, and we will believe in him. [43] He trusts in God. Let God rescue him now if he wants him, for he said, 'I am the Son of God.'" [44] In the same way the rebels who were crucified with him also heaped insults on him.

[45] From noon until three in the afternoon darkness came over all the land. [46] About three in the afternoon Jesus cried out in a loud voice, "Eli, Eli, lema sabachthani?" (which means "My God, my God, why have you forsaken me?").

[47] When some of those standing there heard this, they said, "He's calling Elijah."

[48] Immediately one of them ran and got a sponge. He filled it with wine vinegar, put it on a staff, and offered it to Jesus to drink. [49] The rest said, "Now leave him alone. Let's see if Elijah comes to save him."

[50] And when Jesus had cried out again in a loud voice, he gave up his spirit. (Matthew 27:32–50 NIV)

• What are the key sights, sounds, smells, tastes, and feelings that this passage evokes for you?

Sights

Sounds

Smells

Tastes

Feelings

• How does it affect you to know that Jesus went through this on your behalf?

• What light does this passage shed on your experiences of rejection? Does it offer any encouragement?

2. Do you find it hard to trust God with your deepest needs? How does reflecting on the cross affect your willingness to trust Him?

Lord, You are teaching me so much about trusting You. Fully. Completely. Without suggestions or projections I'm choosing to embrace the very next thing You show me. I'll take this first step. And then I'll take the next.

I finally understand I don't have to fully understand each thing that happens for me to trust You. I don't have to try and figure it out, control it, or even like it for that matter. In the midst of uncertainties, I will just stand and say, "I trust You, Lord."

I visualize me taking my fear of rejection from my incapable clutches and placing my trust in Your full capability. And as I do, I make this all less about me and more about You. I replace my fragile efforts to control with Your fortified realities.

You are the perfect match for my every need.

I am weak. You are strength.

I am unable. You are capability.

I am hesitant. You are assurance.

I am desperate. You are fulfillment.

I am confused. You are confidence.

I am tired. You are rejuvenation.

Though the long path is uncertain, You are so faithful to shed just enough light for me to see the very next step. I now understand this isn't You being mysterious. This is a great demonstration of Your mercy.

Too much revelation and I'd pridefully run ahead of You. Too little and I'd be paralyzed with fear. So, I'm seeking slivers of light in Your Truth just for today and filling the gaps of my unknown with trust.

Uninvited, pages 65–66

3. Pray aloud the prayer from the *Uninvited* book above. Or write your own prayer based on your experience with the story of Jesus' crucifixion.

   Lord Jesus, You were willing to undergo terrible rejection and suffering for my sake. Thank You for Your boundless love, and for . . .

Please also strengthen me with power through Your Spirit in my inner being. Please root and ground me in love, so that I can grasp how wide and long and high and deep Your love is, even though it surpasses knowledge, so that I may be filled with Your fullness.

DAY 6: READ AND LEARN

Continue to make notes about entering situations in God's fullness or your own emptiness on pages 48–49.

Read chapter 8 of the *Uninvited* book, "The Corrective Experience." Use the space below to note any insights or questions you want to bring to the next group session.

The Yoke of God Is Freedom

Attention, Intention, Prevention

GROUP DISCUSSION:

Checking In (9 minutes)

If your group meets for two hours, allow 15 minutes for this discussion.

Welcome to Session 3 of *Uninvited*. A key part of getting to know God better is sharing your journey with others. Before watching the video, briefly check in with one another about your experience since the last session. For example:

- What insights did you discover in the personal study or in chapters 6–8 of the *Uninvited* book?

- How did the last session affect your daily life or your relationship with God?

VIDEO:

The Yoke of God Is Freedom (16 minutes)

Play the video segment for Session 3. As you watch, use the outline provided to follow along or to take additional notes on anything that stands out to you.

Notes

This week's statement to hold on to: Attention, Intention, Prevention

King David was no stranger to rejection. His father assumed that any of his other sons was more likely to be royal material than David (1 Samuel 16:1–13). He was overlooked by man but handpicked by God. Then King Saul drove David out of his court and set about trying to kill him as a rival.

David's men were also no strangers to rejection (1 Samuel 22:1–2).

David got furious at a wealthy landowner named Nabal who rejected him. The man's wife, Abigail, intervened to stop David from killing Nabal and his men. Nabal then died by God's decree, and David married Abigail because he so admired the way she had handled the tense situation (1 Samuel 25:2–44).

David overreacted to Nabal's rejection and was about to step out of God's will to take revenge. When Nabal said, "Who is this son of Jesse?" that triggered David's mind to pull the rejection from his past into this present situation. He was enraged to the point of killing someone. But Abigail intervened. She gave David three gifts in her speech:

• Attention (1 Samuel 25:25)

• Intention (1 Samuel 25:26–27)

• Prevention (1 Samuel 25:30–31)

Puwqah or *puqah* (Hebrew): qualm of conscience, heavy burden of regret

We, too, need to watch where we pay Attention, remember our true Intention, and enter into Prevention.

David at some point learned that instead of wearing the yoke of rejection, he could wear the yoke of the Lord's freedom and live in fullness. Late in his life, when a man pursued him with curses, he had a humble reaction without vengefulness (2 Samuel 16:5–14).

Psalm 23: With God there is fullness. There is no lack. Nothing can be added or subtracted by human acceptance or rejection. With the fullness of God we're free to let humans be humans and let God be God.

The peace of our soul doesn't rise and fall with unpredictable people or situations. The peace of our soul is tethered to all that God is.

GROUP DISCUSSION:

Video Debrief (5 minutes)

1. What part of the teaching had the most impact on you?

Attention, Intention, Prevention (10 minutes)

If your group meets for two hours, allow 20 minutes for this discussion.

2. In the video, Lysa pointed out how Abigail got David to shift his attention from the wrong thing to something better. What did she tell him *not* to pay attention to (1 Samuel 25:25)? What did she want him to pay attention to instead?

   • Think of a time when you felt rejected. You can review your notes on pages 25–26 and 45. What were you paying attention to?

   • What should you have been paying attention to?

3. Abigail got David to refocus on his real intention in the situation (1 Samuel 25:26–27). What was his real intention? What wasn't really his intention?

   • Remember a time where you reacted poorly to a rejection you experienced. Think about your original intention. What happened to that intention once you were rejected? Did the emotion of the situation make you say or think things that you otherwise would have never expressed?

(*For example:* You intended to give and receive love in a relationship. Instead, when that person rejected you, you spewed hurtful things about him or her on social media. Or, even if you didn't post those things on social media, maybe you entertained those hurtful thoughts about the person. Your intention wasn't to ever say or think those hurtful things, but rejection's pain sidetracked your real intention.)

4. Abigail's third gift to David was to move him toward prevention. What did she prevent him from doing (1 Samuel 25:30–31)? Why was that so important not just to her but to him also?

   • David's reaction to rejection was anger and desire for revenge. What emotions did you have when you were rejected? How did you need to be prevented from acting on those emotions?

   • Abigail got David to think about what the consequences of his actions might be. What are some consequences you can think of that may help you not react this way in the future?

Shepherded: What Does the Bible Say? (10 minutes)

If your group meets for two hours, allow 20 minutes for this discussion.

5. Psalm 23 (NIV) embodies a God-focused response to rejection. Read through the psalm and identify how each part addresses the experience of rejection. Refer to the box on page 63 for information about the needs of sheep, and think about how those needs parallel your own needs.

¹The LORD is my shepherd, I lack nothing.

Example: People's rejection doesn't destroy me because in God I have everything I need to flourish.

² He makes me lie down in green pastures,
he leads me beside quiet waters,
    ³ he refreshes my soul.

He guides me along the right paths
    for his name's sake.

⁴ Even though I walk
    through the darkest valley,
I will fear no evil,
    for you are with me;

your rod and your staff,
    they comfort me.

A sheep can't be trained to lie down the way a dog can be. Sheep lie down only when they have had sufficient food and water, are not in danger from predators, and are not afflicted by biting insects.

Sheep can graze on the dry, brown grass of summer, but the best grazing land is green grass near a source of still water. Green grass is available in Israel for about three months a year, so this ideal food source is a rare blessing.

Sheep won't drink from a swiftly flowing stream. They are afraid of rushing water, so the shepherd has to find still water or dig a dead-end channel off from a stream, where still water will pool.

Grazing land often has many faint trails worn down by countless flocks over the years, and sheep easily stray onto the wrong path. A good shepherd goes looking for them and leads them back onto the right path toward home.

It would be terribly dangerous to try to lead sheep through one of the many narrow, deeply cut ravines in Israel. They could easily drown in an unexpected rush of water unless the shepherd knows of a safe trail through the area.

The shepherd's rod is a weapon to protect the sheep from thieves and wild animals. It is about two and a half feet long with bits of iron embedded in the head. The shepherd's staff is longer with a crook in one end, and is used to guide the sheep. It can also hook a lamb to lift it out of danger.[2]

---

[2] Kenneth E. Bailey, *The Good Shepherd: A Thousand-Year Journey from Psalm 23 to the New Testament* (Downers Grove, IL: IVP Academic, 2014), 37–52.

6. What helps you say Psalm 23:1 with conviction—"The LORD is my shepherd; I lack nothing" (NIV)?

[Abigail] spoke her words of truth in the tone of grace. After all, remember David was leading a mob of four hundred men with drawn swords to kill Nabal and all the males who belonged to him. And there were two hundred others who had stayed back to watch the supplies but were just as thirsty for a bloody revenge. But that's not who David was at his core. David was a man who belonged to God. So she spoke to who he was, not how he was acting in the moment:

- You are a fighter of the Lord's battles. (*You are known. You matter to the Lord.*)

- The Lord has a plan for your dynasty to last. (*You are important.*)

- Someone is pursuing you to take your life, but God has a plan to keep you safe. (*You are valuable.*)

- Remember what God did when you hurled that stone from the pocket of a sling toward Goliath. God was faithful that day and is faithful this day too! (*You are secure.*)

Abigail soothed the deep wound Nabal had reopened.

In counseling terms this is called "the corrective experience." She revisited the hurt place of David's heart with healing words that corrected or rewrote the lies that had wounded him so deeply.

Uninvited, page 100

OPTIONAL INDIVIDUAL ACTIVITY AND DISCUSSION:

Redirecting Attention (20 minutes)

If your group meets for two hours, include this activity as part of your meeting. Allow 20 minutes total—5 minutes for the individual activity and 15 minutes for the group discussion.

Individual Activity (5 minutes)

Complete this activity on your own.

1. Spend a few minutes pouring out your heart to God on paper about an experience of rejection that is still painful for you. Tell God what you feel, where your attention is,

what your intention was, and how that worked out. Tell God what you need from Him in this painful place.

Group Discussion (15 minutes)

1. Share what you wrote with the group, to the extent that you feel comfortable doing so.

2. Abigail didn't just give David encouragement; she gave him loving correction for the purpose of his protection. Think about this quote Lysa recently posted on social media: "A wise friend's loving correction is really a gift of protection." How does this speak to you?

3. What do you need most from God in this situation? How could He take you to a place where you're ready to *deal* with hurt instead of *dwelling* on hurt?

Becoming a Group that Lives Loved (8 minutes)

If your group meets for two hours, allow 18 minutes for this discussion.

7. Briefly reflect on what you've learned and experienced together in *Uninvited* so far.

   • Since the first session, how have you experienced God's grace in connection with your feelings of rejection?

   • What shifts do you notice in yourself in terms of how you relate to the group? For example, do you feel more or less guarded, understood, challenged, encouraged, connected, etc.?

INDIVIDUAL ACTIVITY:

What I Want to Remember (2 minutes)
Complete this activity on your own.

1. Briefly review the outline and any notes you took.
2. In the space below, write down the most significant thing you gained in this session—from the teaching, activities, or discussions.

   What I want to remember from this session . . .

(If you want to share what you're learning and see what others are saying about *Uninvited* on social media, use the hashtag #Uninvitedbook!)

CLOSING PRAYER

Close your time together with prayer. Share your prayer requests with one another. Ask God to be your shepherd, supplying your deepest needs, filling you with His fullness in green pastures and still waters, guiding you through the valleys of darkness, defending you with His rod against anyone or anything that would harm you.

Personal Study

DAY 1: STUDY AND REFLECT

1. You can redeem any rejection with the promises of God. Here's how.

   In the left column below, write down feelings you have related to rejection. (If necessary, see the sample list of feelings on page 46.) Then in the right column below, write out a promise from Scripture that counteracts that feeling. Some sample promises you can look up and choose among are listed below, or you can find others with your own search of the Scriptures.

Corrective Experience Chart

FEELING	PROMISE FROM SCRIPTURE
Example:	
Unwanted	*For you are a people holy to the Lord your God. Out of all the peoples on the face of the earth, the Lord has chosen you to be his treasured possession. (Deuteronomy 14:2 NIV)*
	Other possibilities: *Psalm 34:5–9, 18; Psalm 37:4; Psalm 91:1; Isaiah 43:1–3; Isaiah 61; Zephaniah 3:17; John 15:7; Romans 8:31–39; Philippians 1:6; Hebrews 13:5–6*

FEELING	PROMISE FROM SCRIPTURE

2. Choose one of the promises you identified above. Write it somewhere you will see it multiple times a day. Read it to yourself, aloud if possible, several times each day for the next week.

Let your past rejection experiences work *for* you instead of *against* you by allowing them to help you sense the possible pain behind other people's reactions. Try to see things from their vantage point and think of how they might be hurting in this situation. Even if you don't agree with their stance or their reaction, find a way to identify with their hurt. Most people are walking around with way more hurts from their past than we can ever imagine. Pretty much everyone has at some point been deeply hurt by someone. That's your "me too."

Then make a list of good things you know to be true about them. This doesn't validate their actions in the moment, but it will validate their worth as a person. Even if you are clueless about the past hurts that could be feeding their reaction, you can still be sensitive to their obvious pain. You will be an agent of grace in their life as you whisper, "You do belong."

And all of this will help you to stop the cycle of rejection and hurt.

In their life.

And in your life.

Uninvited, pages 101–102

3. Read the excerpt from the *Uninvited* book above. Identify one person who has hurt you, and put into practice what the excerpt recommends. What pain might lie behind this person's reactions?

• What good things can you list about that person?

• How does listing these things affect the way you view that person?

DAY 2: READ AND LEARN

Read chapter 9 of the *Uninvited* book, "Why Does Rejection Hurt So Much?" Use the space below to note any insights or questions you want to bring to the next group session.

DAY 3: STUDY AND REFLECT

I guess this is at the core of why rejection stings in waves over and over again. There's a loss of what was and what we thought would be. What was normal is snatched, and no amount of screaming and running down a sidewalk will get it back.

And it's not just the thing taken that haunts us. It's the reality that humans can be vicious and selfish and cruel.

That's what rejection does. Rejection steals the security of all we thought was beautiful and stable and leaves us scared and fragile and more vulnerable than ever.

Uninvited, pages 80–81

1. David was unflinchingly honest with God about his pain over rejection. Honesty with God was one of the main ways he worked through the pain so he could come out the other side and act in godly ways toward others. Consider what he says here in Psalm 55:

> [4] My heart is in anguish within me;
>   the terrors of death have fallen on me.
> [5] Fear and trembling have beset me;
>   horror has overwhelmed me.
> [6] I said, "Oh, that I had the wings of a dove!
>   I would fly away and be at rest.
> [7] I would flee far away
>   and stay in the desert;
> [8] I would hurry to my place of shelter,
>   far from the tempest and storm." . . .
> [12] If an enemy were insulting me,
>   I could endure it;
> if a foe were rising against me,
>   I could hide.
> [13] But it is you, a man like myself,
>   my companion, my close friend,
> [14] with whom I once enjoyed sweet fellowship
>   at the house of God,
> as we walked about
>   among the worshipers.
> [15] Let death take my enemies by surprise;
>   let them go down alive to the realm of the dead,
>   for evil finds lodging among them.
> [16] As for me, I call to God,
>   and the LORD saves me.
> [17] Evening, morning and noon
>   I cry out in distress,
>   and he hears my voice.
> [18] He rescues me unharmed
>   from the battle waged against me,
>   even though many oppose me.
> [19] God, who is enthroned from of old,
>   who does not change—
> he will hear them and humble them,
>   because they have no fear of God.
> [20] My companion attacks his friends;
>   he violates his covenant.
> [21] His talk is smooth as butter,
>   yet war is in his heart;

> his words are more soothing than oil,
> yet they are drawn swords.
> [22] Cast your cares on the LORD
> and he will sustain you;
> he will never let
> the righteous be shaken. (Psalm 55:4–8, 12–22 NIV)

- What emotions does David express in this psalm?

- What desire is he expressing when he says, "Oh, that I had the wings of a dove!" (v. 6)?

- David says rejection by a friend is worse than rejection by an enemy (vv. 12–14). Why is that the case? How is it encouraging to you that Scripture addresses this?

- What is David's stance toward God (vv. 16–18, 22)? What does he want from God? What does he do? What does he believe about God? (Remember: as with David, the right place to express our hurts is in our time with God—not everywhere else.)

- What do you find helpful in this psalm as you seek to talk with God about your experiences of rejection?

2. David says harsh words to God about his betrayers. We, too, may express harsh words in prayer as we are coming to terms with a rejection. How do we balance these with Jesus' teaching to love our enemies and pray for those who persecute us?

[43] "You have heard that it was said, 'Love your neighbor and hate your enemy.' [44] But I tell you, love your enemies and pray for those who persecute you, [45] that you may be children of your Father in heaven. He causes his sun to rise on the evil and the good, and sends rain on the righteous and the unrighteous. [46] If you love those who love you, what reward will you get? Are not even the tax collectors doing that? [47] And if you greet only your own people, what are you doing more than others? Do not even pagans do that?" (Matthew 5:43–47 NIV)

3. Sit with Psalm 55:22. Repeat it to yourself several times. Then pour out your heart to God about your experiences of rejection or your fears of rejection. You can pray aloud or write your prayer. Don't worry about complete sentences or eloquent words. Just open your heart, trusting that God wants to hear the uncensored truth of what's going on inside you. Allow Him to come to you with His healing presence and grace. He truly will sustain you as you cast your cares on Him.

DAY 4: READ AND LEARN

Read chapter 10 of the *Uninvited* book, "Her Success Does Not Threaten Mine." Use the space below to note any insights or questions you want to bring to the next group session.

DAY 5: STUDY AND REFLECT

We must speak with honor in the midst of being dishonored.

We must speak with peace in the midst of being threatened.

We must speak of good things in the midst of a bad situation.

We must honor, trust, and believe God and let that reality boss around any contrary feelings.

Remember how we've talked about "living loved" and "bringing the fullness of God" into any situation? This is it. And it's really the only way to get to the place where we can have peace in a situation that doesn't have a storybook ending.

Uninvited, page 73

1. Read the excerpt from the *Uninvited* book above. Think of a relationship where you feel dishonored, threatened, or in a bad situation. How might you speak with honor, peace, and goodness in that relationship? Write down something you could say.

2. On the video, Lysa talked about the yoke of people and the yoke of God. The yoke of people is the weight of their unrealistic expectations, their judgment, and their possible rejection. It's heavy and harsh. But the yoke of God is freedom from all that.

[28] "Come to me, all you who are weary and burdened, and I will give you rest. [29] Take my yoke upon you and learn from me, for I am gentle and humble in heart, and you will find rest for your souls. [30] For my yoke is easy and my burden is light." (Matthew 11:28–30 NIV)

We may wonder how Jesus could call any yoke easy. A yoke is a wooden beam that fastens over the necks of two animals and is then attached to a plow or cart that they must pull. Who wants to have to pull a heavy cart? The fact is, we all have a cart to pull, and the only question is whether we're going to try to pull it alone, whether we're going to try to get people to pull it with us, or whether we're going to be yoked with God to pull it. Pulling it alone is really hard. Pulling it with people is unpredictable, because they have their own expectations and judgments of us, so we're often struggling to please them as we try to pull the cart their way or our way. But yoking ourselves to God and getting into

His rhythm of pulling means that the Lord of the universe is doing more than half the work. That's what makes His yoke easy and His burden light.

• When have you tried to wear the yoke of people and gotten burdened by their unrealistic expectations and their rejection?

• What is a current situation in which you need to take on the yoke of God and pull the cart His way?

3. Jesus is "gentle and humble in heart" (Matthew 11:29 NIV), yet He's not a pushover. Read the following passages.

[1] Another time Jesus went into the synagogue, and a man with a shriveled hand was there. [2] Some of them were looking for a reason to accuse Jesus, so they watched him closely to see if he would heal him on the Sabbath. [3] Jesus said to the man with the shriveled hand, "Stand up in front of everyone."

[4] Then Jesus asked them, "Which is lawful on the Sabbath: to do good or to do evil, to save life or to kill?" But they remained silent.

[5] He looked around at them in anger and, deeply distressed at their stubborn hearts, said to the man, "Stretch out your hand." He stretched it out, and his hand was completely restored. [6] Then the Pharisees went out and began to plot with the Herodians how they might kill Jesus.

[7] Jesus withdrew with his disciples to the lake, and a large crowd from Galilee followed. [8] When they heard about all he was doing, many people came to him from Judea, Jerusalem, Idumea, and the regions across the Jordan and around Tyre and Sidon. [9] Because of the crowd he told his disciples to have a small boat ready for him, to keep the people from crowding him. [10] For he had healed many, so that those with diseases were pushing forward to touch him. [11] Whenever the impure spirits saw him, they fell down before him and cried out, "You are the Son of God." [12] But he gave them strict orders not to tell others about him. (Mark 3:1–12 NIV)

• Describe how Jesus deals with rejection in Mark 3:1–12.

[19] Meanwhile, the high priest questioned Jesus about his disciples and his teaching.

[20] "I have spoken openly to the world," Jesus replied. "I always taught in synagogues or at the temple, where all the Jews come together. I said nothing in secret. [21] Why question me? Ask those who heard me. Surely they know what I said."

[22] When Jesus said this, one of the officials nearby slapped him in the face. "Is this the way you answer the high priest?" he demanded.

[23] "If I said something wrong," Jesus replied, "testify as to what is wrong. But if I spoke the truth, why did you strike me?" (John 18:19–23 NIV)

- Describe how Jesus deals with rejection in John 18:19–23, which takes place shortly after Jesus is arrested.

- How would you compare Jesus' responses to rejection with David's in 1 Samuel 25?

- Based on this comparison, how could you go about being "gentle and humble in heart" without being passive?

4. Read Isaiah 26:3–4 in several versions below.

> [3] You keep him in perfect peace
>   whose mind is stayed on you,
>   because he trusts in you.
> [4] Trust in the LORD forever,
>   for the LORD GOD is an everlasting rock. (ESV)

> [3] You will keep in perfect peace
>   those whose minds are steadfast,
>   because they trust in you.
> [4] Trust in the LORD forever,
>   for the LORD, the LORD himself, is the Rock eternal. (NIV)

> People with their minds set on you,
>> you keep completely whole,
> Steady on their feet,
>> because they keep at it and don't quit.
> Depend on GOD and keep at it
>> because in the LORD GOD you have a sure thing. (MSG)

• How does each version describe a mind that's at peace?

• Why is a steadfast mind essential when we go into situations where we might feel rejected?

• How can this passage nourish you as you seek to bring the fullness of God into the situations you face?

• How does *The Message* (MSG) interpret the idea of trust in God? Why is this an appropriate way to think about trust?

5. Pray for God's easy yoke.

God, You are gentle and humble in heart, even when people reject You. You never get vengeful, and You don't crawl away into a corner. You stay engaged and forgiving. That's the way I want to be. Please give me Your yoke. I don't want to wear the yoke of people's expectations anymore. And I don't want to keep trying to do life by myself. I want to be yoked to You. Please show me how to . . .

DAY 6: READ AND LEARN

Read chapter 11 of the *Uninvited* book, "Ten Things You Must Remember When Rejected." Which one of these can you live out this week? Use the space below to note any insights or questions you want to bring to the next group session.

Set Apart

I'm not set aside; I'm set apart.

GROUP DISCUSSION:

Checking In (10 minutes)

If your group meets for two hours, allow 15 minutes for this discussion.

Welcome to Session 4 of *Uninvited*. A key part of getting to know God better is sharing your journey with others. Before watching the video, briefly check in with one another about your experience since the last session. For example:

- What insights did you discover in the personal study or in chapters 9–11 of the *Uninvited* book?
- How did the last session affect your daily life or your relationship with God?

VIDEO:

Set Apart (13 minutes)

Play the video segment for Session 4. As you watch, use the outline provided to follow along or to take additional notes on anything that stands out to you.

Notes

We need to fight to keep trusting God even when circumstances beg us to be suspicious of God.

This week's statement to hold on to: I'm not set aside; I'm set apart.

Prayers answered with "no" or "wait" can make you feel unnoticed, uninvited. But as you pray through those feelings, see if your situation has more to do with you being prepared than with you being overlooked.

Hannah felt provoked and irritated. Her anguish was so intense that she wouldn't eat. But she wasn't set aside. She was set apart.

We desperately want something and see the Lord blessing other women in that area. We feel set aside. Why them and not us? If God is good, why isn't He being good to us in this?

Hannah was the first person to have individual prayer in the sanctuary.

God's delay in answering Hannah's prayer was protection for a high calling, not a rejection. First, Hannah was set apart to be a model of fervent prayer even for Jewish men. She stood alone, determined, intently concentrated on her task, filled with deep faith and a sense of mission. This is what Jewish people try to imitate.

Second, Hannah was set apart to pray a thanksgiving song that became a model for Jesus' mother, Mary (compare 1 Samuel 2:1–11 to Luke 1:46–55).

Third, Hannah was set apart to be the mother of Samuel, who played a vital role in Israel's transition from the time of the judges to the time of the kings of Israel.

Hannah's answer to prayer didn't come right away. It came "in the course of time" (1 Samuel 1:20 NIV).

GROUP DISCUSSION:

Video Debrief (5 minutes)

1. What part of the teaching had the most impact on you?

Fervent Prayer: What Does the Bible Say? (15 minutes)

If your group meets for two hours, allow 25 minutes for this discussion.

2. Read aloud 1 Samuel 1:1–20. In Hannah's day, a woman's worth was measured by her ability to bear sons for her husband. So in addition to her own natural desire for children, she had to bear the burden of her whole society's expectations.

[1]There was a certain man from Ramathaim, a Zuphite from the hill country of Ephraim, whose name was Elkanah son of Jeroham, the son of Elihu, the son of Tohu, the son of Zuph, an Ephraimite. [2]He had two wives; one was called Hannah and the other Peninnah. Peninnah had children, but Hannah had none.

[3] Year after year this man went up from his town to worship and sacrifice to the LORD Almighty at Shiloh, where Hophni and Phinehas, the two sons of Eli, were priests of the LORD. [4] Whenever the day came for Elkanah to sacrifice, he would give portions of the meat to his wife Peninnah and to all her sons and daughters. [5] But to Hannah he gave a double portion because he loved her, and the LORD had closed her womb. [6] Because the LORD had closed Hannah's womb, her rival kept provoking her in order to irritate her. [7] This went on year after year. Whenever Hannah went up to the house of the LORD, her rival provoked her till she wept and would not eat. [8] Her husband Elkanah would say to her, "Hannah, why are you weeping? Why don't you eat? Why are you downhearted? Don't I mean more to you than ten sons?"

[9] Once when they had finished eating and drinking in Shiloh, Hannah stood up. Now Eli the priest was sitting on his chair by the doorpost of the LORD's house. [10] In her deep anguish Hannah prayed to the LORD, weeping bitterly. [11] And she made a vow, saying, "LORD Almighty, if you will only look on your servant's misery and remember me, and not forget your servant but give her a son, then I will give him to the LORD for all the days of his life, and no razor will ever be used on his head."

[12] As she kept on praying to the Lord, Eli observed her mouth. [13] Hannah was praying in her heart, and her lips were moving but her voice was not heard. Eli thought she was drunk [14] and said to her, "How long are you going to stay drunk? Put away your wine."

[15] "Not so, my lord," Hannah replied, "I am a woman who is deeply troubled. I have not been drinking wine or beer; I was pouring out my soul to the LORD. [16] Do not take your servant for a wicked woman; I have been praying here out of my great anguish and grief."

[17] Eli answered, "Go in peace, and may the God of Israel grant you what you have asked of him."

[18] She said, "May your servant find favor in your eyes." Then she went her way and ate something, and her face was no longer downcast.

[19] Early the next morning they arose and worshiped before the LORD and then went back to their home at Ramah. Elkanah made love to his wife Hannah, and the LORD remembered her. [20] So in the course of time Hannah became pregnant and gave birth to a son. She named him Samuel, saying, "Because I asked the LORD for him." (1 Samuel 1:1–20 NIV)

• What sorts of provoking things might Peninnah have been saying to Hannah?

• How would you describe Hannah's attitude toward God in the midst of her pain?

- What might Hannah have said and done if her rejection had made her suspicious of God?

- In what ways was Hannah set apart, not set aside? How was she being prepared, not overlooked?

- Why is it important for us to note that Hannah's prayer was not answered immediately but "in the course of time"?

To be set aside is to be rejected.

That's exactly what the enemy would have wanted me to feel. If he could get me to feel this, then I'd become completely self-absorbed in my own insecurity and miss whatever the reason God had for me to be at this event.

To be set apart is to be given an assignment that requires preparation.

That's what I believe God wanted me to see. . . .

The lesson was this: anything that infuses us with humility is good. Even if it feels a bit like humiliation in the moment, the workings of humility within are a gift. . . .

The Bible reminds us that on the other side of humility we find wisdom (Proverbs 11:2). We will be lifted up by God Himself in due time (1 Peter 5:6). God opposes the proud but gives grace to the humble (James 4:6). Humility isn't a place of weakness but rather a position that will come with honor (Proverbs 18:12). And humility is an absolute requirement for those who ask God to heal their land (2 Chronicles 7:14).

Uninvited, pages 109, 111

3. Read the excerpt from the *Uninvited* book on page 83. What do you feel are the differences between humiliation and humility?

• Look up Proverbs 11:2. Why do you think humility is essential for wisdom?

• Why do you think God opposes the proud?

• How did Hannah demonstrate humility?

When God Says No (15 minutes)

If your group meets for two hours, allow 25 minutes for this discussion.

4. What are the things you've prayed for passionately and haven't yet received?

5. How do you deal with these prayers to which God has said "no" or "wait"?
   ☐ I'm still asking persistently.
   ☐ I've buried this desire in my heart and tried to move on.
   ☐ I've decided that God has said no, and I'm trying to be at peace with that.
   ☐ I'm frustrated that God isn't responding.
   ☐ I'm blaming myself for the lack of an answer.
   ☐ Other (describe it):

6. How do you view God in light of these prayers to which He hasn't said "yes"? Have you grown at all suspicious of Him, doubting His love for you? Or do you have some other view of Him?

- What possible good may come from your having to wait for the answers to your prayers? How could you grow? What is one good thing you can learn? How could others benefit?

- What might God be setting you apart for? If you don't know, what can you do to go about finding out?

- What do you need to do to boost your courage so that you keep moving forward with God and your life despite this setback?

7. Be committed as a group to fill the waiting space with prayer. How can the group pray for you in this situation? Do you need prayer support for things such as humility, patience, and courage while you wait for your prayers to be answered?

   Write down how you are going to pray for the other members of your group.

NAME	PRAYER REQUEST

NAME	PRAYER REQUEST

Decide you'll only ask questions that help you move forward instead of feeling stuck in the reasons this happened. "What" questions increase our ability to become more self-aware, while "why" questions only focus on things out of our control. . . .

Questions that I've found helpful:

What is one good thing I've learned from this?

What was a downside to this situation that I can be thankful is no longer my burden to carry?

What were the unrealistic expectations I had, and how can I better manage these next time?

What do I need to do to boost my courage to pursue future opportunities?

What is one positive change I could make in my attitude about the future?

What are some lingering negative feelings about this situation that I need to pray through and shake off to be better prepared to move forward?

What is one thing God has been asking me to do today to make tomorrow easier?

Uninvited, pages 136–137

OPTIONAL INDIVIDUAL ACTIVITY AND DISCUSSION:

What vs. Why (20 minutes)

If your group meets for two hours, include this activity as part of your meeting. Allow 20 minutes total—5 minutes for the individual activity and 15 minutes for the group discussion.

Individual Activity (5 minutes)

Complete this activity on your own.

1. Choose one experience of rejection or one prayer in which you're waiting for breakthrough. Then read the questions excerpted from the *Uninvited* book on page 86. Ask yourself one of those questions and write your response. If you have time, write your response to another of those questions.

Group Discussion (15 minutes)

1. Share what you wrote with the group, to the extent that you feel comfortable doing so.

2. Did you find the questions helpful? Why or why not?

3. Did anyone else's answers give you insight as to how you might answer that question for yourself? If so, how?

4. How is it more productive to ask "What" questions like these than to ask "Why is this happening to me? Why has God allowed it? Why is He blessing someone else and not me?"

INDIVIDUAL ACTIVITY:

What I Want to Remember (2 minutes)

Complete this activity on your own.

1. Briefly review the outline and any notes you took.
2. In the space below, write down the most significant thing you gained in this session—from the teaching, activities, or discussions.

   What I want to remember from this session . . .

(If you want to share what you're learning and see what others are saying about *Uninvited* on social media, use the hashtag #Uninvitedbook!)

CLOSING PRAYER

Close your time together with prayer. Refer back to question 7 on page 85, where you talked about how the group could pray for you. Take time to pray for each person in the ways she asked to be prayed for. Ask God to hear your prayers and fulfill them in the course of time as will be best for you.

Personal Study

1. Do you avoid some situations out of a fear of rejection? Maybe you don't go to that large group gathering where you might be lonely in a crowd. Maybe you don't join the women's group at church, or maybe you avoid contact with the family members who have rejected you in the past. Write down the names of people, organizations, and types of events that you avoid because you don't want to risk rejection.

2. When have your decisions to avoid people and situations been wise, and when have they simply narrowed your life?

3. What do you want to say to God about your stance of avoiding people and situations, if you have such a stance? Is there anything you would like help on to be able to act differently? Or have you wisely learned to avoid hurtful people and choose friends who are available and compatible?

4. Choose a person you avoid because you fear rejection, or because this person has made it clear that he or she doesn't want to have contact with you. What good things could you ask God to do for this person? Try to come up with at least six good things.

• Write a prayer to God for this person. Ask God to bless this person's life, to do good *in* them and *for* them. Ask Him to deal with this person according to His grace, not according to what the person deserves. Ask God also to completely cleanse your heart from resentment toward this person.

5. Whenever you feel the fear of rejection, you can remember Colossians 3:12:

Therefore, as God's chosen people, holy and dearly loved, clothe yourselves with compassion, kindness, humility, gentleness and patience. (NIV)

You are chosen and dearly loved by God, and holy (set apart) for His high purposes. The foundation of this identity can enable you to clothe yourself in good ways of treating other people. What feelings or thoughts come into your mind when you think about being chosen?

DAY 2: READ AND REFLECT

Read chapter 12 of the *Uninvited* book, "The Enemy's Plan Against You." Use the space below to note any insights or questions you want to bring to the next group session.

DAY 3: STUDY AND REFLECT

Whatʼs a brokenhearted person to do? We must praise Him, seek Him, look to Him, call to Him, experience Him, fear Him, learn from Him, honor Him, draw near to Him, and take refuge in Him.

This is how we take back control from something or someone that was never meant to have it and declare God as Lord. . . .

Rejection doesn't label you. It enables you to adjust and move on.

Fill in the blank: This rejection doesn't mean I'm ____ [whatever negative label or shame-filled feeling you are having] _____ . It makes this ___ [opportunity] [person] [desire] _____ a wrong fit for me right now. Instead of letting the feelings from this situation label me, I'm going to focus on God and His promises for good things.

Psalm 34:5: "Those who look to him are radiant; their faces are never covered with shame" [NIV].

Uninvited, pages 130–132

1. Prayer that isn't answered the way we'd like it to be—or any perceived rejection—doesn't just cause us to doubt God. It also often causes us to doubt or label ourselves. We may undervalue ourselves and think the problem is that we are unworthy of asking for the thing we long for. We may label ourselves as:

Disqualified	Not important enough
Unworthy	Not good enough
Foolish	Insignificant
Selfish	Too demanding
Isolated	Left out

When we label ourselves like this, we orchestrate a rejection by God, when in reality He isn't rejecting us at all. He's merely waiting to answer our prayer at the best time, or He's saying no because that will be best for us in the long run.

What label(s) are you tempted to put on yourself because of an unsatisfied prayer or a painful rejection?

2. Fill in the blanks below to make a God-centered statement about that experience.

This rejection or unsatisfied prayer doesn't mean I'm _____

_____ (whatever negative label or shame-filled feeling you are having). It makes this _____ (opportunity) (person) (desire) a wrong fit for me right now. Instead of letting the feelings from this situation label me, I'm going to focus on God and His promises for good things.

3. Read that statement aloud. How does it make you want to respond?

4. When you cry out to God, He's delighted that you're pursuing Him. He takes pleasure in your company and is overjoyed when you are depending on Him. Read the following promises He makes in Psalm 34 and underline one that speaks especially to your heart.

> 5 Those who look to him are radiant;
>   their faces are never covered with shame.
> 6 This poor man called, and the LORD heard him;
>   he saved him out of all his troubles.
> 7 The angel of the LORD encamps around those who fear him,
>   and he delivers them.
> 8 Taste and see that the LORD is good;
>   blessed is the one who takes refuge in him.
> 9 Fear the LORD, you his holy people,
>   for those who fear him lack nothing. . . .
> 18 The LORD is close to the brokenhearted
>   and saves those who are crushed in spirit. (vv. 5–9, 18 NIV)

• What is it about that promise that is especially meaningful to you?

5. Pray a prayer of thanksgiving based on the verse you chose. For example, *Thank You, God, that You are close to the brokenhearted, because that means You are close to me. I need You to . . .*

DAY 4: READ AND REFLECT

Read chapter 13 of the *Uninvited* book, "Miracles in the Mess." Use the space below to note any insights or questions you want to bring to the next group session.

DAY 5: STUDY AND REFLECT

1. Competition between wives was a common occurrence in Old Testament times. Hannah and Peninnah weren't the only wives to have strife related to child-bearing. Read Genesis 29:31–30:24. Leah and Rachel were sisters married to the same man. Rachel was the beautiful one, and her husband loved her, but God gave children to Leah, not Rachel. How did Rachel handle this situation of being seemingly rejected by God?

• 30:1–2

• 30:3–8

- 30:14–16 (mandrakes were supposed to aid fertility)

2. How do you think Rachel should have dealt with the situation?

3. Is there a relationship or situation in your life where you're tempted to react negatively because you feel rejected by God or another person? If so, how do you deal with it? (For example, consider the way you respond to social media posts. Do you ever feel threatened or rejected by something someone posts?)

4. Consider your very next social media post. Will it encourage or discourage others? How can you make sure it encourages others and doesn't come from the "Rachel" in you?

5. Praising God is a great way to get into a positive frame of mind. Pray aloud Psalm 34:1–4, and then use it as a springboard to your own prayer for God's fullness and freedom from your fears.

> ¹I will extol the LORD at all times;
>   his praise will always be on my lips.
> ²I will glory in the LORD;
>   let the afflicted hear and rejoice.
> ³Glorify the LORD with me;
>   let us exalt his name together.
> ⁴I sought the Lord, and he answered me;
>   he delivered me from all my fears. (NIV)

• What are the specific fears you need to be delivered from? Ask God, and trust that He will answer that prayer.

DAY 6: READ AND LEARN

Read chapter 14 of the *Uninvited* book, "Moving Through the Desperate In-Between." Use the space below to note any insights or questions you want to bring to the next group session.

Remembering God's Presence

Resisting God's promises will make us forget God's presence. But resting in God's promises, and reciting God's promises, will help us remember God's presence.

GROUP DISCUSSION:

Checking In (10 minutes)

If your group meets for two hours, allow 15 minutes for this discussion.

Welcome to Session 5 of *Uninvited*. A key part of getting to know God better is sharing your journey with others. Before watching the video, briefly check in with one another about your experience since the last session. For example:

- What insights did you discover in the personal study or in chapters 12–14 of the *Uninvited* book?

- How did the last session affect your daily life or your relationship with God?

VIDEO:

Remembering God's Presence (24 minutes)

Play the video segment for Session 5. As you watch, use the outline provided to follow along or to take additional notes on anything that stands out to you.

Notes

This week's statement to hold on to: Resisting God's promises will make us forget God's presence. But resting in God's promises, and reciting God's promises, will help us remember God's presence.

"Who then is the one who condemns? No one. Christ Jesus who died—more than that, who was raised to life—is at the right hand of God and is also interceding for us" (Romans 8:34 NIV). Jesus talks to the Father on our behalf from the point of view of one who knows rejection.

Amidst the healing and teaching in Mark 5–6 we find Mark 5:40, "They laughed at him." And Mark 6:3, "they took offense at him" (NIV). Messy realities in the midst of the miracles.

The terrified disciples didn't understand the miracle of the loaves because "their hearts were hardened" (Mark 6:52 NIV). The word "hardened" here means "unresponsive, completely lacking sensitivity or spiritual perception."

The disciples had witnessed expressions of God, but they hadn't turned those expressions into personal experiences. We can go to Bible study and *amen* every point made, but if we don't apply it to our lives we won't be changed. Inspiration and information without personal application will never amount to transformation.

Romans 12:2 reminds us to be transformed by the renewing of our minds. This is the shift in thinking we've been talking about, operating out of fullness and living loved despite whatever circumstances may be surrounding us.

Anyplace where we have hardened our hearts or refused to let truth touch and transform that part of us, there will be confusion.

"Terrified" in Mark 6:50 (NIV) is *tarasso*, which means: "to set in motion what needs to remain still."

Searching for acceptance outside of God's presence can lead us to some dangerous places.

Jesus isn't running from your mess. He's climbing into the boat with you.

Here are some good questions to ask ourselves:

- Information » Have I sought out God's truth regarding this situation?
- Application » Have I applied God's truth without compromise to this situation?
- Transformation » Do I now own this truth as a personal revelation from God to use in future situations like this?

GROUP DISCUSSION:

Video Debrief (5 minutes)

1. What part of the teaching had the most impact on you?

Reflecting on the Miracle: What Does the Bible Say? (10 minutes)

If your group meets for two hours, allow 20 minutes for this discussion.

2. Read aloud Mark 6:30–52.

   [30] The apostles gathered around Jesus and reported to him all they had done and taught. [31] Then, because so many people were coming and going that they did not even have a chance to eat, he said to them, "Come with me by yourselves to a quiet place and get some rest."

   [32] So they went away by themselves in a boat to a solitary place. [33] But many who saw them leaving recognized them and ran on foot from all the towns and got there ahead of them. [34] When Jesus landed and saw a large crowd, he had compassion on them, because they were like sheep without a shepherd. So he began teaching them many things.

   [35] By this time it was late in the day, so his disciples came to him. "This is a remote place," they said, "and it's already very late. [36] Send the people away so that they can go to the surrounding countryside and villages and buy themselves something to eat."

   [37] But he answered, "You give them something to eat."

   They said to him, "That would take more than half a year's wages! Are we to go and spend that much on bread and give it to them to eat?"

   [38] "How many loaves do you have?" he asked. "Go and see."

   When they found out, they said, "Five—and two fish."

   [39] Then Jesus directed them to have all the people sit down in groups on the green grass. [40] So they sat down in groups of hundreds and fifties. [41] Taking the five loaves and the two fish and looking up to heaven, he gave thanks and broke the loaves. Then he gave them to his disciples to distribute to the people. He also divided the two fish among them all. [42] They all ate and were satisfied, [43] and the disciples picked up twelve basketfuls of broken pieces of bread and fish. [44] The number of the men who had eaten was five thousand.

   [45] Immediately Jesus made his disciples get into the boat and go on ahead of him to Bethsaida, while he dismissed the crowd. [46] After leaving them, he went up on a mountainside to pray.

   [47] Later that night, the boat was in the middle of the lake, and he was alone on land. [48] He saw the disciples straining at the oars, because the wind was against them. Shortly before

dawn he went out to them, walking on the lake. He was about to pass by them, [49] but when they saw him walking on the lake, they thought he was a ghost. They cried out, [50] because they all saw him and were terrified.

Immediately he spoke to them and said, "Take courage! It is I. Don't be afraid." [51] Then he climbed into the boat with them, and the wind died down. They were completely amazed, [52] for they had not understood about the loaves; their hearts were hardened. (Mark 6:30–52 NIV)

• Why did Jesus lead the disciples away to a remote place (vv. 30–31)?

• Why did Jesus change His plans (v. 34)?

• What should the disciples have learned about Jesus from these motivations of His?

• What should they have learned about Him from His feeding of the five thousand?

• What would they have done differently on the lake if they had learned these lessons and applied them to their lives?

3. Read the passage on the feeding again (vv. 35–44). Try to picture and hear the scene in your mind. What small details jump out at you as you reflect deeply on the story?

• What does Jesus want you to learn and take to heart from this story, so that you don't have a hardened heart about it?

• What would you do differently in your life if you truly applied this insight to yourself?

• Why might you resist applying this story to your life?

• What encourages you to follow through with the application of this story to your life?

Resting in the Promises (10 minutes)

If your group meets for two hours, allow 25 minutes for this discussion.

4. Many of the promises of Scripture are meant for all believers. Below is a series of promises. Read each one and tell what it would mean for you to *rest* in that promise or *resist* that promise.

Who then is the one who condemns? No one. Christ Jesus who died—more than that, who was raised to life—is at the right hand of God and is also interceding for us. (Romans 8:34 NIV)

• How would your life be different if you truly rested in Romans 8:34 and applied it?

• Why might someone resist Romans 8:34?

[1] Do not fear, for I have redeemed you;
    I have summoned you by name; you are mine.
[2] When you pass through the waters,
    I will be with you;
and when you pass through the rivers,
    they will not sweep over you.
When you walk through the fire,
    you will not be burned;
    the flames will not set you ablaze.
[3] For I am the LORD your God,
    the Holy One of Israel, your Savior. (Isaiah 43:1–3 NIV)

• How would your life be different if you truly rested in Isaiah 43:1–3 and applied it?

• Why might someone resist Isaiah 43:1–3?

[11] "For I know the plans I have for you," declares the LORD, "plans to prosper you and not to harm you, plans to give you hope and a future. [12] Then you will call on me and come and pray to me, and I will listen to you. [13] You will seek me and find me when you seek me with all your heart." (Jeremiah 29:11–13 NIV)

• How would your life be different if you truly rested in Jeremiah 29:11–13 and applied it?

• Why might someone resist Jeremiah 29:11–13?

And my God will meet all your needs according to the riches of his glory in Christ Jesus. (Philippians 4:19)

• How would your life be different if you truly rested in Philippians 4:19 and applied it?

• Why might someone resist Philippians 4:19?

> [5] Keep your lives free from the love of money and be content with what you have, because God has said,
> > "Never will I leave you;
> > > never will I forsake you."
> [6] So we say with confidence,
> > "The Lord is my helper; I will not be afraid.
> > > What can mere mortals do to me?" (Hebrews 13:5–6 NIV)

• How would your life be different if you truly rested in Hebrews 13:5–6 and applied it?

• Why might someone resist Hebrews 13:5–6?

If any of you lacks wisdom, you should ask God, who gives generously to all without finding fault, and it will be given to you. (James 1:5 NIV)

- How would your life be different if you truly rested in James 1:5 and applied it?

- Why might someone resist James 1:5?

5. Which of these promises do you most need to take to heart right now?

6. Ephesians 4:22–24 says, "You were taught, with regard to your former way of life, to put off your old self, which is being corrupted by its deceitful desires; to be made new in the attitude of your minds; and to put on the new self, created to be like God in true righteousness and holiness" (NIV). What are some ways you can put off the old and put on the new?

7. What will help you rest in the promise you chose in question 5, despite the temptation to resist it?

What happened yesterday can't be changed, but it can be forgiven. That's your miracle in the mess.

The voices of condemnation, shame, and rejection can come at you, but they no longer have to reside in you. That's your miracle in the mess.

And the temptations that were so hard to resist in your flesh will be overpowered by your truth-transformed mind. That's your miracle in the mess.

Uninvited, page 170

OPTIONAL INDIVIDUAL ACTIVITY AND DISCUSSION:

Information, Application, Transformation (20 minutes)

If your group meets for two hours, include this activity as part of your meeting. Allow 20 minutes total—5 minutes for the individual activity and 15 minutes for the group discussion.

In a messy situation, these are three good questions to ask:

- Information » Have I sought out God's truth regarding this situation?
- Application » Have I applied God's truth without compromise to this situation?
- Transformation » Do I now own this truth as a personal revelation from God to use in future situations like this?

Individual Activity (5 minutes)

Complete this activity on your own.

1. Identify and describe a messy situation you are facing.

2. What is God's truth regarding this situation? If you don't know, are you comfortable asking the group for help? If not, why not?

3. If you do know God's truth regarding the situation, have you applied it without compromise? If so, how? If not, why not?

Group Discussion (15 minutes)

1. What was it like for you to ask yourself those questions? Helpful? Uncomfortable? Something else? Why?

2. Ask the group for help in clarifying God's truth regarding your messy situation. See if you can help one another identify passages of Scripture that speak to each person's situation. If you still don't have clarity, who else can you ask?

3. Which is more challenging for you: identifying the right information about God's truth or putting that truth into practice with a good application? Why do you think that's the case?

4. What makes you hopeful in a messy situation?

INDIVIDUAL ACTIVITY:

What I Want to Remember (2 minutes)

Complete this activity on your own.

1. Briefly review the outline and any notes you took.
2. In the space below, write down the most significant thing you gained in this session—from the teaching, activities, or discussions.

   What I want to remember from this session . . .

(If you want to share what you're learning and see what others are saying about *Uninvited* on social media, use the hashtag #Uninvitedbook!)

CLOSING PRAYER

Close your time together with prayer. How can the group pray for you? For example, are you in a messy situation that you would like the group to pray about? Do you need God's help to rest in a promise? Is it going to be challenging for you to put into practice what God is saying to you through the feeding of the five thousand?

Personal Study

DAY 1: STUDY AND REFLECT

1. Lysa told a story about setting things into motion that were supposed to stay still. Those choices led to a pregnancy and an abortion. When has fear led you to set things into motion that should have stayed still?

2. The past can't be changed, but it can be forgiven. What would you like to say to God right now about what you wrote in question 1?

3. In what current circumstance do you need to take to heart Jesus saying, "Take courage! It is I. Don't be afraid" (Mark 6:50 NIV)?

4. Choose a Scripture promise from pages 102–104 or one of those below.

> Your own ears will hear him.
>> Right behind you a voice will say,
> "This is the way you should go,"
>> whether to the right or to the left. (Isaiah 30:21 NLT)

[6] Do not be anxious about anything, but in every situation, by prayer and petition, with thanksgiving, present your requests to God. [7] And the peace of God, which transcends all understanding, will guard your hearts and your minds in Christ Jesus. (Philippians 4:6–7 NIV)

If we confess our sins, he is faithful and just and will forgive us our sins and purify us from all unrighteousness. (1 John 1:9 NIV)

- What does this promise mean for your life? What difference does it make to the way you will live? How does it affect your world?

- Copy the promise somewhere you'll see it multiple times each day, such as on your phone. Recite it to yourself and then take a few minutes to rest in it and think about it. Revisit your thoughts on how the promise affects your world at that very moment.

5. Each evening this week, take a few minutes to review the day. Have you rested in your chosen promise? When were you resting in it, and when weren't you? Follow this pattern:

   a. **Become aware of God's presence.** Ask God to be present with you. Ask Him for clarity and understanding about your day, which at first may seem like a blur.

   b. **Review your day with gratitude.** Before you consider how you interacted with God's promise today, notice the day's joys. Walk through your day with God and take note of the small things to be grateful for. Look at the people you interacted with—what did you give to them and what did you receive from them? What tasks did you accomplish? Think about what you ate and what you saw. What were the day's small gifts?

   c. **Reflect on God's promise.** Now notice those moments when you were resting in God's promise and those moments when you weren't. Take some notes below. Over time, you may discern a pattern. What emotions went along with resting? With not resting?

   d. **Pray about your promise.** Ask God to forgive the ways in which you fell short and to enable you to rest in His promise more deeply tomorrow. Ask for imperfect progress. Read your promise aloud, and thank God for it. Pay attention to the feelings that arise as you think about the day to come. Allow those emotions to become the basis for prayer. Ask for guidance, understanding, help, and hope.

*L*ord, *draw me close.*

Your Word promises when I draw close to You, You are there. I want my drawing close to be a permanent dwelling place. At any moment when I feel weak and empty and alone, I pray that I won't let those feelings drag me down into a pit of insecurity. But rather, I want those feelings to be triggers for me to immediately lift those burdensome feelings to You and trade them for the assurance of Your security.

I am not alone, because You are with me. I am not weak, because Your strength is infused in me. I am not empty, because I'm drinking daily from Your fullness. You are my dwelling place. And in You I have shelter from every stormy circumstance and harsh reality. I'm not pretending the hard things don't exist, but I am rejoicing in the fact that Your covering protects me and prevents those hard things from affecting me like they used to.

You, the Most High, the name above every rejection, have the final say over me. You know me and love me intimately and personally and fully. Let my reactions to all things make it so evident that I spend a lot of time with You. I want my gentleness to be evident to all. I want Your fullness in me to be the atmosphere around me. I want Your love to shine through me. And I want Your peace to be the path I walk. Your truth to be my wisdom when I talk. You are my everyday dwelling place, my saving grace.

Uninvited, pages 178–179

DAY 2: READ AND LEARN

Read chapter 15 of the *Uninvited* book, "I Want to Run Away." Use the space below to note any insights or questions you want to bring to the next group session.

Also, take a few minutes at the end of the day to review the day. This is a time to gently notice what happened. Follow this pattern:

- Become aware of God's presence.

- Review your day with gratitude.

- Reflect on God's promise.

- Pray about your promise.

DAY 3: STUDY AND REFLECT

I **want a promise for my problem of feeling empty.**

> "Man does not live on bread alone but on every word that comes from the mouth of the LORD" (Deuteronomy 8:3 NIV).

My soul was hand designed to be richly satisfied in deep places by the Word of God. When I go without the nourishment of truth, I will crave filling my spiritual hunger with temporary physical pleasures, thinking they will somehow treat the loneliness inside. These physical pleasures can't fill me, but they can numb me. Numb souls are never growing souls. They wake up one day feeling so very distant from God and wondering how in the world they got there.

Since Satan's goal is to separate us from the Lord, this is exactly where he wants us to stay. But the minute we turn to His Word is the minute the gap of distance between us and God is closed. He is near always. His Word is full and fully able to reach those deep places inside us desperate for truth.

I want a promise for my problem of feeling deprived.

> "Fear the LORD your God, serve him only and take your oaths in his name" (Deuteronomy 6:13 NIV). Another version of this verse says, "Worship Him, your True God, and serve Him" (THE VOICE).

When we worship God, we reverence Him above all else.

A great question to ask myself: *Is my attention being held by something sacred or something secret?* What is holding my attention the most is what I'm truly worshiping.

Sacred worship is all about God.

Secret worship is all about something in this world that seems so attractive on the outside but will devour you on the inside.

Pornography, sex outside of marriage, trading your character to claw your way to a position of power, fueling your sense of worth with your child's successes, and spending outside of your means to constantly dress your life in the next new thing—all things we do to counteract feelings of being left out of and not invited to the good things God has given others—these are just some of the ways lust sneaks in and wreaks havoc. Two words that characterize misplaced worship or lust are *secret excess.*

God says if we will direct our worship to Him, He will give us strength to turn from the mistakes of yesterday and provide portions for our needs of today. "Whom have I in heaven but you? / And earth has nothing I desire besides you. / My flesh and my heart may fail, / but God is the strength of my heart / and my portion forever" (Psalm 73:25–26 NIV).

And I certainly want a promise for my problem of feeling rejected.

"Do not put the LORD your God to the test." (Deuteronomy 6:16 NIV).

At first glance I don't understand why Jesus chose Deuteronomy 6:16 to combat rejection. And it almost makes me doubt this third part has anything to do with it. But then it stirs my heart so wonderfully when I tuck it back in the context of the other verses around it. Verses 13–15 remind us, "Fear the LORD your God, serve him only and take your oaths in his name. Do not follow other gods, the gods of the peoples around you; for the LORD your God, who is among you, is a jealous God" (NIV).

He is jealous for you. He is jealous for me. The fullness of His love and lavish acceptance is the only match for the rejections we will experience. And He absolutely doesn't want us making other relationships the false gods of our worship. As we seek love and acceptance, God doesn't want us to test Him, just trust Him.

When He says we are holy and dearly loved children, we must trust that this is true. Studying these three promises proclaimed by Jesus has absolutely captured my heart.

Uninvited, pages 155–158

1. Read the three promises in the excerpt from *Uninvited* on pages 112–113. Do you need a promise for feeling empty, deprived, or rejected? What does each of these passages say to you?

   Man does not live on bread alone but on every word that comes from the mouth of the LORD. (Deuteronomy 8:3 NIV)

   • What place has the Word of God had in your life today?

   • How has that affected your day?

Worship Him, your True God, and serve Him. (Deuteronomy 6:13 THE VOICE)

• What has dominated your attention today? God? Something else?

• How has that affected your day?

Do not put the LORD your God to the test. (Deuteronomy 6:16 NIV)

• How does God's value of you outweigh the rejections you may get from people?

2. At the end of the day, take a few minutes to review the day. Follow this pattern:

a. **Become aware of God's presence.** Ask God to be present with you. Ask Him for clarity and understanding about your day, which at first may seem like a blur.

b. **Review your day with gratitude.** Before you consider how you interacted with God's promise today, notice the day's joys. Walk through your day with God and take note of the small things to be grateful for. Look at the people you interacted with—what did you give to them and what did you receive from them? What tasks did you accomplish? Think about what you ate and what you saw. What were the day's small gifts?

c. **Reflect on God's promise.** Now notice those moments when you were resting in God's promise and those moments when you weren't. Take some notes below. Over time, you may discern a pattern. What emotions went along with resting? With not resting?

d. Pray about your promise. Ask God to forgive the ways in which you fell short and to enable you to rest in His promise more deeply tomorrow. Ask for imperfect progress. Read your promise aloud, and thank God for it. Pay attention to the feelings that arise as you think about the day to come. Allow those emotions to become the basis for prayer. Ask for guidance, understanding, help, and hope.

DAY 4: READ AND LEARN

Read chapter 16 of the *Uninvited* book, "What I Thought Would Fix Me Didn't." Use the space below to note any insights or questions you want to bring to the next group session.

Also, take a few minutes at the end of the day to review the day. Follow this pattern:

• Become aware of God's presence.

• Review your day with gratitude.

• Reflect on God's promise.

• Pray about your promise.

DAY 5: STUDY AND REFLECT

1. In the chart below, record opportunities this week when you rested in and recited God's promises to remember His presence.

SITUATION	PROMISE I RECITED	HOW THE PROMISE HELPED ME	HOW I WALKED IN GOD'S FULLNESS
Example: My child was acting out at a store.	Philippians 4:6–7	It helped me keep my temper in check.	I disciplined my child without raging or inwardly fuming. I was able to stay in touch with my love for my child even while saying no to him.

2. Do you notice any patterns in the times when you are resting in God's promise and the times when you forget about it or resist it? If so, when are the good times and when are the hard times? Are you alone or with people? Which people? Are there particular activities that distract you or make you more resistant to God's promise?

3. What would help you rest in God's promise more than you are? Would reading it more often help? What about checking in with a friend each day to share where you are regarding your promise? What about building into your day some two-minute breaks when you refocus on God's love for you and His promise to you?

How do we invite God into this desperate in-between?

We invite His closeness.

For me, this means praying. But sometimes when my heart feels hurt and empty, my words feel quite flat at best, nonexistent at worst. When I feel hurt, I get quiet. So, to keep my prayers from feeling forced and insincere, I pray Psalm 91.

It won't take the rejection away. But it will help us press through it. And give us something healthy with which to fill the desperate in-between. No matter how vast our pit, prayer is big enough to fill us with the realization of His presence like nothing else.

I hope with every part of me you'll dare to whisper these ten simple prayers I've written. Fill that empty space with truths tender enough for this raw place. Let His reassurance reset your atmosphere. Let His miraculous mercies wrap their way around you. Let His words of life breathe fresh air into those deep choking places. And determine to inhale life, fully, deeply, completely once again.

Use these prayers in whatever way is most helpful for you. They could be all strung together in one sitting. Or, you can use them individually for the next five days, praying one in the morning and another at night.

Uninvited, pages 177–178

4. Pray through Psalm 91. You may use the written prayers on pages 178–186 of the *Uninvited* book or say your own prayer. Write your prayer below or in a journal or say it aloud.

DAY 6: READ AND REFLECT

Read the bonus chapter from the *Uninvited* book. Use the space below to note any insights or questions you want to bring to the next group session.

Lessons from the Olive

The oil is coming, and where there is oil, there is the potential for light.

GROUP DISCUSSION:

Checking In (10 minutes)

If your group meets for two hours, allow 15 minutes for this discussion.

Welcome to Session 6 of *Uninvited*. A key part of getting to know God better is sharing your journey with others. Before watching the video, briefly check in with one another about your experience since the last session. For example:

- What insights did you discover in the personal study or in chapters 15, 16, and the bonus chapter of the *Uninvited* book?

- How did the last session affect your daily life or your relationship with God?

VIDEO:

The Oil Is Coming (20 minutes)

Play the video segment for Session 6. As you watch, use the outline provided to follow along or to take additional notes on anything that stands out to you.

Notes

This week's statement to hold on to: The oil is coming, and where there is oil, there is the potential for light.

Jesus knew the heart-crushing feeling of rejection in the Garden of Gethsemane. He knew He was ultimately alone in His assignment.

Jesus could have run away, but instead He said to His Father, "Yet not what I will, but what you will" (Mark 14:36 NIV).

Jesus is the light of life (John 1:1–5).

Jesus chose to spend this time of wrestling in an olive grove. There are three important lessons from the olive:

• First, olive trees need both the harsh east wind and the refreshing west wind.

• Second, olives have to be heavily processed in order to get rid of hardness and bitterness and become useful.

- Third, in order to produce valuable oil, the olive has to be pressed. The oil can then produce light.

We don't lose heart because the hard pressing we are experiencing won't crush us (2 Corinthians 4:6-9, 16–18).

As long as Lysa kept wishing that her past was different, she remained stuck being hurt by her father's rejection. But if she really believed that the hard times could produce something good—as when the olive is pressed—then she could trust God's plan. Do you have a rejection that has left you bitter?

Jesus modeled this when He said, "Yet not what I will, but what you will."

Pray, "Lord, I trust that in all things Your will is good, and I can trust You even when I don't understand. You clearly promise that when I'm blinded by all these dark realities of life, You will guide me through. You will help me see provisions. And Lord, I ask You to help me to be humble enough to receive all that You want me to receive. You will make the rough places smooth, and You will never forsake me."

> I will lead the blind by ways they have not known,
> along unfamiliar paths I will guide them;
> I will turn the darkness into light before them
> and make the rough places smooth.
> These are the things I will do;
> I will not forsake them. (Isaiah 42:16 NIV)

The facts of our past don't define the destiny of our future.

GROUP DISCUSSION:

Video Debrief (5 minutes)

1. What part of the teaching had the most impact on you?

In Gethsemane: What Does the Bible Say? (10 minutes)

If your group meets for two hours, allow 20 minutes for this discussion.

2. Read aloud Mark 14:32–42. Gethsemane means "oil press" or "the place where oil is pressed." Jesus led His disciples there after the Last Supper, when He knew that Judas had gone to bring the men who would arrest Him.

[32] They went to a place called Gethsemane, and Jesus said to his disciples, "Sit here while I pray." [33] He took Peter, James and John along with him, and he began to be deeply distressed and troubled. [34] "My soul is overwhelmed with sorrow to the point of death," he said to them. "Stay here and keep watch."

[35] Going a little farther, he fell to the ground and prayed that if possible the hour might pass from him. [36] "Abba, Father," he said, "everything is possible for you. Take this cup from me. Yet not what I will, but what you will."

[37] Then he returned to his disciples and found them sleeping. "Simon," he said to Peter, "are you asleep? Couldn't you keep watch for one hour? [38] Watch and pray so that you will not fall into temptation. The spirit is willing, but the flesh is weak."

[39] Once more he went away and prayed the same thing. [40] When he came back, he again found them sleeping, because their eyes were heavy. They did not know what to say to him.

[41] Returning the third time, he said to them, "Are you still sleeping and resting? Enough! The hour has come. Look, the Son of Man is delivered into the hands of sinners. [42] Rise! Let us go! Here comes my betrayer!" (Mark 14:32–42 NIV)

• What was Jesus' emotional state at this time (vv. 33–34)?

• Why did Jesus feel this way?

• What did He mean when He asked His Father, "Take this cup from me" (v. 36)?

• Why were His words, "Yet not what I will, but what you will" so significant? What was He saying, and why did it matter so much?

• How are these words remarkable, given Jesus' emotional state? What are people with such emotions more often inclined to say to God?

- Jesus was honest about His emotions and still prayed, "Yet not what I will, but what you will." Have you ever been in a situation where you needed to be honest about your emotions and yet pray for God's will? If so, what was—or is—that situation?

- Lysa prayed, "Yet not what I will, but what you will" about her father's rejection of her. She prayed it to let go of wanting to change her past. What events of your past do you need to let go of in this way?

- Part of letting go and not letting rejection define you is to allow it to develop you and direct you to Jesus. How do you see this being worked out in your life?

- What are the benefits that come from praying this prayer and meaning it?

- Take time to pray the prayer on page 125 together. Jesus was alone in the garden with His pain while His disciples slept, but you have each other, and He is right in your midst.

Yet not what I will, but what you will.

I trust that in all these things, Your will is good. I can trust You even when I don't understand. I cannot fully trust You while still holding on to things that made me question You.

You so clearly promise when I am blinded by the dark realities, You will guide me. You will guide me to the spiritual help I need. But You will also guide me to the emotional and physical help I need. Help me see Your provisions and be humble enough to receive them. You will make the rough places smooth. You will do these things and will never forsake me.

You have said, "I will lead the blind by ways they have not known, / along unfamiliar paths I will guide them; / I will turn the darkness into light before them / and make the rough places smooth. / These are the things I will do; / I will not forsake them" (Isaiah 42:16 NIV).

You say Your Word is sharper than a double-edged sword. So I cut these ties from my soul with the precise edge of Your truth.

I was abandoned. That is a fact from my past, but it is not the destiny of my future.

I was rejected. That is a fact from my past, but it is not the destiny of my future.

I was hurt. That is a fact from my past, but it is not the destiny of my future.

I was left out. That is a fact from my past, but it is not the destiny of my future.

I was brokenhearted. That is a fact from my past, but it is not the destiny of my future.

Heartbreaking seasons can certainly grow me but were never meant to define me. I let go of the hurt and embrace the growth the minute I'm able to say, "Yet not what I will, but what you will."

Uninvited, pages 197–198

Lessons from the Olive (10 minutes)

If your group meets for two hours, allow 25 minutes for this discussion.

3. What life lessons can we learn from each of the following facts about the olive?

• In order to be fruitful, the olive tree needs both the harsh east wind from the desert and the refreshing west wind from the sea.

- The olive is too hard and bitter to eat in its natural state. To become edible, it has to be washed, broken, soaked, and sometimes salted. This all takes time.

- The most valuable part of the olive, the oil, comes only when the olive is pressed and pressed again.

4. How are these life lessons relevant in your life? Where would you say you are in the process? Explain your answer.

  ☐ Right now I'm feeling the harsh desert wind.

  ☐ I'm enjoying the refreshing wind from the sea.

  ☐ I'm being washed.

  ☐ I'm being soaked.

  ☐ I'm being broken open.

  ☐ I'm being salted.

  ☐ I'm being hard pressed to produce oil.

  ☐ Other: _____

5. Read aloud 2 Corinthians 4:6–9, 16–18.

> [6] For God, who said, "Let light shine out of darkness," made his light shine in our hearts to give us the light of the knowledge of God's glory displayed in the face of Christ.
>
> [7] But we have this treasure in jars of clay to show that this all-surpassing power is from God and not from us. [8] We are hard pressed on every side, but not crushed; perplexed, but not in despair; [9] persecuted, but not abandoned; struck down, but not destroyed. . . .
>
> [16] Therefore we do not lose heart. Though outwardly we are wasting away, yet inwardly we are being renewed day by day. [17] For our light and momentary troubles are achieving for us an eternal glory that far outweighs them all. [18] So we fix our eyes not on what is seen, but on what is unseen, since what is seen is temporary, but what is unseen is eternal. (2 Corinthians 4:6–9, 16–18 NIV)

• How have we experienced light (v. 6)? What is the light we've experienced?

• How have you experienced what verses 8–9 describe?

• What reasons for not losing heart does Paul give in verses 16–18?

• What helps you see your troubles as light and momentary?

• What are the unseen realities that Paul wants us to fix our eyes on?

6. What does it mean when Lysa says: "The oil is coming, and where there is oil, there is the potential for light"?

• How is this statement true in your life? What do you want to do about it?

We're forever out of breath in hot pursuit of becoming someone we perceive we need to be:

"One day I'll become someone's wife."

"One day I'll become someone significant."

"One day I'll live there or drive that or be able to buy things without looking at the price tags."

"One day I'll hit this benchmark of success or brilliance or status."

We say it with such confidence and then chase everything and everyone that can help make this happen. And in the process we run further and further away from the only Giver of good gifts. The One who wants to live a love story with us. Not as the magic genie we occasionally run to for a little dose of divine help. But the One who stills us, quiets us, wipes away our exhaustion, and whispers:

"It's not about you *becoming* anything. Your soul was made to simply *be* with Me. And the more you are with Me, the more you will stop fearing what the world might take from you. With Me you are free to be you. The real you. The you honesty called to at the very beginning of this journey. The you whose core is in alignment with My truth. The you who doesn't fear imperfections or rejections, because grace has covered those in the loveliest of ways."

Overcoming rejection can never be dependent on overcoming a perceived obstacle. "I want that, and if I get it life will be great." No. Oh, God, cripple the part of our hearts that dares misguide us with this thinking.

The deepest part of me runs to find honesty. And when I find honesty, I realize it was Jesus calling to me all along.

Uninvited, pages 207–209

OPTIONAL GROUP DISCUSSION:

Choosing Good Goals (20 minutes)

If your group meets for two hours, include this discussion as part of your meeting.

1. Read the excerpt from the *Uninvited* book above. What dream or desire captivates your soul and feels like something you need in order to be fulfilled? Or what has been that enticing dream or desire for you in the past?

   One day I'll _____

2. How do we go about breaking free from placing so much of our identity in this dream or desire?

3. What is one good dream or desire you have that doesn't entice you away from simply being yourself with Jesus?

4. Allow three minutes to sit together in silence with this Scripture verse:

> For God alone my soul waits in silence;
> from him comes my salvation. (Psalm 62:1 ESV)

Use the silent time to give your dreams and desires to God and to reflect on waiting in silence for God alone. The group leader can read the verse aloud slowly a couple of times as you begin. Afterward, share what those few minutes were like for you.

INDIVIDUAL ACTIVITY:

What I Want to Remember (2 minutes)

Complete this activity on your own.

1. Briefly review the outline and any notes you took.

2. In the space below, write down the most significant thing you gained in this session— from the teaching, activities, or discussions.

What I want to remember from this session . . .

(If you want to share what you're learning and see what others are saying about *Uninvited* on social media, use the hashtag #Uninvitedbook!)

CLOSING PRAYER

Close your time together with prayer. Focus your prayer on the things for which you are grateful in this group. What gifts have the other members of the group given you? What have you gained from the study? How has God been present to you? Give everyone a chance to voice at least one thing she is grateful for.

Personal Study

DAY 1: STUDY AND REFLECT

Sometimes we experience suffering and we interpret it as rejection from God. But suffering is common in this fallen world, and God allows us to go through it even though He loves us deeply. We are like olives being pressed to produce oil, and the oil will come if we stay focused on God and His goodness. This day's questions are designed to help you reframe your experiences of suffering as something other than rejection from God.

1. How have you experienced suffering over the course of your life? Think about physical and emotional challenges. Think of pain as a parent, a spouse, at school, in the work-place, in church, in friendships, etc.

Suffering I faced as a child:

Suffering I faced as a teen:

Suffering I have faced as an adult:

2. Choose one experience of suffering you mentioned above. How did you get through it?

3. How did your choice influence the way that experience ultimately affected you and your outlook on life?

4. Looking back, what oil (a source of light) has God brought out of the pressure of your suffering? For example, character growth, faith, compassion for others, ministry, increased desire for God, or the inclination to pray more.

5. We get to choose whether we let a time of suffering make us bitter or better. Which choice have you made? What's the evidence?

6. If you've chosen bitterness in the past, you can make a new start today. Tell God about your bitterness and ask Him to empower you with His Spirit in your inner being to walk away from that bitterness and choose a new future. Ask Him to root and ground you in His love so that you can forgive anyone involved in your suffering, and so that you can let go of blaming God or yourself. Pour out your heart to Him until all that old bitterness washes away in the cleansing of truth.

DAY 2: STUDY AND REFLECT

Rejection never has the final say. Rejection may be a delay or distraction or even a devastation for a season. But it's never a final destination. I'm destined for a love that can't ever be diminished, tarnished, shaken, or taken. With You, Jesus, I'm forever safe. I'm forever accepted. I'm forever held. Completely loved and always invited in.

Uninvited, page 209

1. When we have this confidence that we're forever safe with Jesus, the rejections that do come along won't destroy us, so we don't have to live in fear of rejection. We can begin to make sense of the Bible's insistence that trials—including rejections—can be a source of joy. Read James 1:2–4:

   ²Consider it pure joy, my brothers and sisters, whenever you face trials of many kinds, ³because you know that the testing of your faith produces perseverance. ⁴Let perseverance finish its work so that you may be mature and complete, not lacking anything. (NIV)

   • What reasons does James give for considering trials an opportunity for joy?

   • What is perseverance? Why is it so valuable?

   • How important is it to you to become mature and complete as a follower of Christ? Honestly, just between you and God. Is it worth a little rejection? Or not really?

2. Read 2 Corinthians 1:3–7:

[3] All praise to God, the Father of our Lord Jesus Christ. God is our merciful Father and the source of all comfort. [4] He comforts us in all our troubles so that we can comfort others. When they are troubled, we will be able to give them the same comfort God has given us. [5] For the more we suffer for Christ, the more God will shower us with his comfort through Christ. [6] Even when we are weighed down with troubles, it is for your comfort and salvation! For when we ourselves are comforted, we will certainly comfort you. Then you can patiently endure the same things we suffer. [7] We are confident that as you share in our sufferings, you will also share in the comfort God gives us. (NLT)

- How does the apostle Paul say the process of suffering and comfort works? What does God do? What do we do?

- Have you experienced comfort from God? If so, how?

- We talked about resting in God's promises several weeks ago. What do you think about resting in this promise: "For the more we suffer for Christ, the more God will shower us with his comfort through Christ" (v. 5)? What draws you to that promise? Or what pushes you away?

- Some people would rather be immune from suffering than have to depend on God's comfort. Why is that an ultimately unwise attitude?

• Do you need comfort from God right now? Go to Him. Be with Him. Let down all your walls and tell Him exactly what is on your mind. Let yourself be in the place of needing Him. Be completely yourself—with no pretending.

DAY 3: STUDY AND REFLECT

On the other side of being pressed and crushed is oil . . . the most valuable part of me set free to emerge.

On the other side of every hardship is a resurrection.

We must believe that what God has said He will do will be done. Don't focus on the problems. Instead, have the resurrection mind-set that holds fast to God's promises. Good is coming!

This was true for Jesus. It's true for the olive tree. And it's certainly true for you and me as well. Though my circumstances may not change today, my outlook surely can. I will not run. I will rise above. I will trust God's will above my desires. I will let truth free my soul from ties to past hurts. I will step into today's destiny. And in the doing of this, I see His flicker of light, and a pulse of divine hope courses through my heart.

Uninvited, pages 201–202

1. What progress do you see in yourself since you first began the study in the following areas?

Living loved

Bringing the fullness of God into situations instead of your own emptiness

Watching where you pay Attention, remembering your true Intention, and entering into any necessary Prevention

Acting like you're set apart

Resting in God's promises

2. Which of these practices do you need to revisit even after the study ends?

3. Have you committed any promises to memory, or have you developed a habit of reciting a promise to yourself often throughout the day? If so, what difference has that promise made in your life?

4. Here is one final promise you can take with you. What does Isaiah 41:9–10 promise you?

> [9] I took you from the ends of the earth,
>   from its farthest corners I called you.
> I said, "You are my servant";
>   I have chosen you and have not rejected you.
> [10] So do not fear, for I am with you;
>   do not be dismayed, for I am your God.
> I will strengthen you and help you;
>   I will uphold you with my righteous right hand. (NIV)

• How is this promise relevant to your life?

• What difference does it make to the way you live that God has chosen you and not rejected you?

• What difference does it make to your attitudes and actions that God has established a relationship with you ("I am your God")?

• For what do you need His strength as you go forward beyond this study?

5. Offer to God a prayer based on Isaiah 41:9–10.

Lord, thank You for choosing me and not rejecting me, even though I don't come from some-where important but from the ends of the earth. I need to rest in the knowledge that You will never reject me. Thank You for . . .

DAY 4: REVIEW AND RESPOND

If your group is going to have the bonus Session 7 to talk about what you've learned and experienced together throughout the *Uninvited* study, use your personal study for the rest of this week to review the previous sessions and identify the teaching, discussions, or activities that stand out most to you.

You may want to review notes from the video teaching, what you wrote down for "What I Want to Remember" at the end of each group session, responses to the personal studies, etc. Consider such questions as:

• What struggles or progress did I experience related to this session?

• What was the most important thing I learned about myself in this session?

• How did I experience God's presence or grace related to this session?

• How did this session affect my relationships with the other people in the group?

Session 1: Living Loved (pages 9–34)

Session 2: Empty or Full? (pages 35–55)

Session 3: The Yoke of God Is Freedom (pages 57–78)

Session 4: Set Apart (pages 79–95)

Session 5: Remembering God's Presence (pages 97–118)

Session 6: Lessons from the Olive (pages 119–140)

Bonus Session: Review and Celebration

This bonus session is a chance for you
to solidify and celebrate what you've learned in *Uninvited*.

GROUP DISCUSSION (45–60 minutes)

1. What, if anything, from Session 6—either the group meeting or the personal study—would you like to comment on? A teaching that encouraged or challenged you? A new insight? An experience since the last meeting that allowed you to put the session's truth into practice?

2. What would you say is the most important thing you have learned or experienced throughout this *Uninvited* study? How has it affected you—for example, in your attitudes, behaviors, or relationships? The six statements to hold on to are below as reminders:

   • Live from a deep assurance that you are fully loved, and you won't find yourself begging others for scraps of love. Live loved.

   • I can choose to bring my emptiness or God's fullness into any situation I face.

   • Attention, Intention, Prevention

   • I'm not set aside, I'm set apart.

- Resisting God's promises will make us forget God's presence. But resting in God's promises, and reciting God's promises, will help us remember God's presence.
- The oil is coming, and where there is oil, there is the potential for light.

3. How have you recognized God at work in your life through the study? For example, how has He helped you live loved or live in His fullness and His presence? What promises has He given you? What challenges has He set before you?

4. Revisit the charts from the Sessions 1 and 2 personal studies (Day 1) in which you journaled about past and current rejections. How have your feelings changed, if at all, toward these people/situations based on the scriptural truths presented throughout this study? In which relationships/situations might you still need to experience God's healing touch?

5. As you've been reminded of your own security in Christ during this study, how will you in turn make the people you daily encounter feel wanted and accepted? What practical things can you do to consistently "feed" and "take care of" Jesus' sheep?

6. What might be God's current invitation to *you* personally? How does that invitation make you feel? Excited? Scared? Explain.

7. How will this study move you forward in your walk with God and your relationships with others?

CLOSING PRAYER (10–15 minutes)

As you end your time together, pray in any of the following directions:

- Offer heartfelt praise to God, celebrating again the wonderful truth that He loves us and has invited us to be part of His family.

- Ask God to continue to heal group members struggling with past rejection and to guide your reactions and subsequent actions each time future experiences of rejection occur.

- Ask God to daily make you sensitive to those who need to be "invited in," who need a word of encouragement or a show of support.

Scripture Index

Session 1

Isaiah 61:1
Matthew 6:26–27
John 15:7
Ephesians 1:4–5
Mark 3:20–22

Luke 4:14–21
Matthew 7:9–12
Psalm 37:4
Isaiah 53:3–5

Matthew 5:1–16
Zephaniah 3:17
Psalm 91:1
Mark 2:23–3:6

Session 2

Luke 22:47–62
Psalm 46:10
Ephesians 1:4–5
Psalm 27:1

John 21:15–17
Philippians 4:12
Romans 8:31
Matthew 27:32–50

Ephesians 3:14–19
Psalm 23:6
Hebrews 13:5b–6

Session 3

1 Samuel 16:1–13
2 Samuel 16:5–14
Romans 8:31
Deuteronomy 14:2
Psalm 91:1
Zephaniah 3:17
Philippians 1:6
Mark 3:1–12

1 Samuel 22:1–2
Psalm 23
Psalm 55:4–8, 12–22
Psalm 34:5–9, 18
Isaiah 43:1–3
John 15:7
Hebrews 13:5–6
John 18:19–23

1 Samuel 25:2–44
Matthew 11:28–30
Matthew 5:43–47
Psalm 37:4
Isaiah 61
Romans 8:31–39
Psalm 55:4–8, 12–22

Session 4

1 Samuel 1:1–20
Proverbs 11:2
Proverbs 18:12
Psalm 34:1–9, 18

1 Samuel 2:1–11
1 Peter 5:6
2 Chronicles 7:14
Genesis 29:31–30:24

Luke 1:46–55
James 4:6
Colossians 3:12

Session 5

Mark 6:48
Mark 6:1–4
Romans 12:1–2
Jeremiah 29:11–13
James 1:5
1 John 1:9
Deuteronomy 8:3

Romans 8:34
Mark 6:30–44
Romans 8:34
Philippians 4:19
Isaiah 30:21
Deuteronomy 6:13–16
Psalm 91

Mark 5:21–42
Mark 6:45–52
Isaiah 43:1–3
Hebrews 13:5–6
Philippians 4:6–7
Psalm 73:25–26

Session 6

Mark 14:32–42
2 Corinthians 4:6–9, 16–18
James 1:2–4

John 18:1–2
Isaiah 42:16
2 Corinthians 1:3–7

John 1:1–5
Psalm 62:1
Isaiah 41:9–10

About the Author

Lysa TerKeurst is a wife to Art and mom to five priority blessings named Jackson, Mark, Hope, Ashley, and Brooke. She is president of Proverbs 31 Ministries and author of seventeen books, including the *New York Times* bestsellers *The Best Yes*, *Unglued*, and *Made to Crave*. Additionally, Lysa has been featured on *Focus on the Family*, *The Today Show*, *Good Morning America*, and more. Lysa speaks nationwide at Catalyst, Women of Faith, and various church events.

To those who know her best, Lysa is simply a carpooling mom who loves Jesus passionately, is dedicated to her family, and struggles like the rest of us with laundry, junk drawers, and cellulite.

WEBSITE:

If you enjoyed *Uninvited*, equip yourself with additional resources at www.uninvitedbook.com, www.LysaTerKeurst.com, and www.Proverbs31.org.

SOCIAL MEDIA:

Connect with Lysa on a daily basis, see pictures of her family, and follow her speaking schedule:

Blog:
www.LysaTerKeurst.com

Facebook:
www.Facebook.com/OfficialLysa

Instagram:
@LysaTerKeurst

Twitter:
@LysaTerKeurst

About Proverbs 31 Ministries

Lysa TerKeurst is the president of Proverbs 31 Ministries, located in Charlotte, North Carolina.

If you were inspired by *Uninvited* and desire to deepen your own personal relationship with Jesus Christ, we have just what you're looking for.

Proverbs 31 Ministries exists to be a trusted friend who will take you by the hand and walk by your side, leading you one step closer to the heart of God through:

Free *First 5* app

Free online daily devotions

Online Bible studies

Writer and speaker training

Daily radio programs

Books and resources

For more information about Proverbs 31 Ministries, visit:
www.proverbs31.org.

To inquire about having Lysa speak at your event, visit
www.LysaTerKeurst.com and click on "speaking."

Free gifts for you!

*You know those desperate moments where life's hurts
and rejections make you feel helpless?*

Infuse God's hope and power into your heart with Lysa's FREE audio recording of "Prayers to Press Through Rejection." Based on Psalm 91, these deeply personal and healing prayers will help you declare God's promises over your life.

Visit www.proverbs31.org/
uninvitedgift to download yours.

Stop allowing rejection to steal the best of who you are with help from the declarations found in "10 Things You Must Remember When Rejected."

Visit www.proverbs31.org/
uninvitedgift to download your FREE printable copy today.

Also Available from Lysa TerKeurst

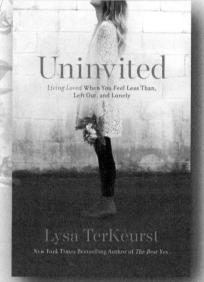

In *Uninvited*, Lysa shares her own deeply personal experiences of rejection—from the perceived judgment of the perfectly toned woman one elliptical over to the incredibly painful childhood abandonment by her father. She leans in to honestly examine the roots of rejection as well as rejection's ability to poison relationships from the inside out, including our relationship with God.

With biblical depth, gut-honest vulnerability, and refreshing wit, Lysa will help you:

- Stop feeling left out by believing that even when you are overlooked by others you are handpicked by God.

- Change your tendency to either fall apart or control the actions of others by embracing God-honoring ways to process your hurt.

- Know exactly what to pray for the next ten days to steady your soul and restore your confidence in the midst of rejection.

- Overcome the two core fears that feed your insecurities by understanding the secret of belonging.

For more information, go to uninvitedbook.com.

Unglued

Making Wise Choices in the Midst of Raw Emotions

Lysa TerKeurst
New York Times *Bestselling Author*

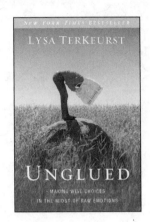

God gave us emotions to experience life, not destroy it! Lysa TerKeurst admits that she, like most women, has had experiences where others bump into her happy and she comes emotionally unglued. We stuff, we explode, or we react somewhere in between. What do we do with these raw emotions? Is it really possible to make emotions work for us instead of against us? Yes, and in her usual inspiring and practical way, Lysa will show you how. Filled with gut-honest personal examples and biblical teaching, *Unglued* will equip you to:

- Know with confidence how to resolve conflict in your important relationships.
- Find peace in your most difficult relationships as you learn to be honest but kind when offended.
- Identify what type of reactor you are and how to significantly improve your communication.
- Respond with no regrets by managing your tendencies to stuff or explode.
- Gain a deep sense of calm by responding to situations out of your control.

Also Available:

Unglued Curriculum

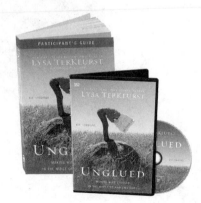

Made to Crave

Satisfying Your Deepest Desire with God, Not Food

Lysa TerKeurst,
New York Times *Bestselling Author*

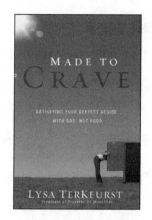

Made to Crave is the missing link between a woman's desire to be healthy and the spiritual empowerment necessary to make that happen. The reality is we were made to crave. Craving isn't a bad thing. But we must realize God created us to crave more of Him. Many of us have misplaced that craving by overindulging in physical pleasures instead of lasting spiritual satisfaction. If you are struggling with unhealthy eating habits, you can break the "I'll start again Monday" cycle, and start feeling good about yourself today. Learn to stop beating yourself up over the numbers on the scale. Discover that your weight loss struggle isn't a curse but rather a blessing in the making, and replace justifications that lead to diet failure with empowering go-to scripts that lead to victory. You can reach your healthy weight goal — and grow closer to God in the process.

Also Available:

Made to Crave Curriculum

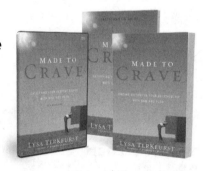

Available in stores and online!

Becoming More Than a Good Bible Study Girl

Lysa TerKeurst,
New York Times *Bestselling Author*

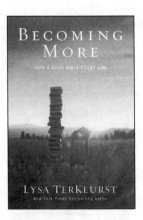

Is Something Missing in Your Life?

Lysa TerKeurst knows what it's like to consider God just another thing on her to-do list. For years she went through the motions of a Christian life: Go to church. Pray. Be nice.

Longing for a deeper connection between what she knew in her head and her everyday reality, she wanted to personally experience God's presence.

Drawing from her own remarkable story of step-by-step faith, Lysa invites you to uncover the spiritually exciting life we all yearn for. With her trademark wit and spiritual wisdom, Lysa will help you:

- Learn how to make a Bible passage come alive in your own devotion time.
- Replace doubt, regret, and envy with truth, confidence, and praise.
- Stop the unhealthy cycles of striving and truly learn to love who you are and what you've been given.
- Discover how to have inner peace and security in any situation.
- Sense God responding to your prayers.

The adventure God has in store for your life just might blow you away.

Also Available:

Becoming More Than a Good Bible Study Girl Curriculum